PRACTICE – ASSESS – DIAGNOSE

180 Days of HIGH-FREQUENCY WORDS for Kindergarten

Authors
Jesse Hathaway, M.S.Ed.

SHELL EDUCATION

For information on how this resource meets national and other state standards, see page 4. You may also review this information by visiting our website at www.teachercreatedmaterials.com/administrators/correlations/ and following the on-screen directions.

Publishing Credits

Corinne Burton, M.A.Ed., *Publisher*; Conni Medina, M.A.Ed., *Managing Editor*; Emily R. Smith, M.A.Ed., *Content Director*; Angela Johnson, M.A.Ed., M.F.A., *Editor*; Lee Aucoin, *Senior Multimedia Designer*; Don Tran, *Production Artist;* Kyleena Harper, *Assistant Editor*

Image Credits

All images from iStock and Shutterstock.

Standards

Shell Education
A division of Teacher Created Materials
5301 Oceanus Drive
Huntington Beach, CA 92649-1030

http://www.tcmpub.com/shell-education

ISBN 978-1-4258-1633-9

Printed in China 51497

TABLE OF CONTENTS

INTRODUCTION AND RESEARCH

If you teach early learners to read, you know how important the mastery of high-frequency words is to reading success. Students who are exposed to and learn high-frequency words during these critical years of academia set the foundation for reading and overall success as scholars. The words in this book make up "65% of written material" that we encounter on a daily basis and are the connective tissues used to craft even the simplest written sentence (Fry 2000, 4).

The Need for Practice

To be successful in today's classroom, students must be able to accurately identify and read high-frequency words. Building accuracy and fluency when reading these words is critical for later reading success mainly because, unlike other words, "some of these often-used words do not follow regular phonics rules" (Fry 2000, 4). Being able to read these words allows students to focus on fluency instead of decoding while reading. The National Reading Panel suggests that repeated exposure to high-frequency words is crucial to reading instruction and sets the building blocks for decoding, fluency, and comprehension (2000). According to Robert Marzano, "practice has always been, and always will be, a necessary ingredient to learning procedural knowledge at a level at which students execute it independently" (2010, 83).

Understanding Assessment

In addition to providing opportunities for frequent practice, teachers must be able to assess students' acquisition of high-frequency words. This is important for teachers to adequately support students' progress in fluency and comprehension. Assessment is a long-term process that often involves careful analysis of students' responses from discussions, projects, practice sheets, and tests. In short, the data gathered from assessments should be used to inform instruction: slow down, speed up, or reteach. This type of evaluation is called *formative assessment* (McIntosh 1997).

HOW TO USE THIS BOOK

180 Days of High-Frequency Words for Kindergarten offers weekly units to guide students as they practice and learn words every day of the school year. Each daily activity is designed to engage students with the words of the week. On the first day, students are introduced to the words of the week. For the rest of the week, students complete activities in which they must **recognize**, **play with**, **use**, and **write** the words of the week.

Easy to Use and Standards Based

The Every Student Succeeds Act (ESSA) mandates that all states adopt challenging academic standards that help students meet the goal of college and career readiness. While many states already adopted academic standards prior to ESSA, the act continues to hold states accountable for detailed and comprehensive standards. These daily activities reinforce grade-level skills and allow students to read, write, speak, and listen to high-frequency words every day of the school year. This chart indicates reading, writing, language, and print concept standards that are addressed throughout this book.

Reading—phonics and word recognition	Read common high-frequency words by sight.
	Distinguish between similarly spelled words by identifying the sounds of the letters that differ.
	Add drawings or other visual displays to descriptions as desired to provide additional detail.
Writing—text type and purpose	Use a combination of drawing, dictating, and writing to compose informative/explanatory texts in which students name what they are writing about and supply some information about the topic.
Language—conventions of standard English	Demonstrate command of the conventions of standard English grammar and usage when writing or speaking.
	Print many uppercase and lowercase letters.
	Use frequently occurring nouns and verbs.
	Produce and expand complete sentences in shared language activities.
	Demonstrate command of the conventions of standard English capitalization, punctuation, and spelling when writing.
	Capitalize the first word.
	Spell simple words phonetically, drawing on knowledge of sound-letter relationships.
Print concepts	Demonstrate understanding of the organization and basic features of print.
	Follow words from left to right, top to bottom, and page by page.
	Recognize that spoken words are represented in written language by specific sequences of letters.
	Understand that words are separated by spaces in print.

HOW TO USE THIS BOOK *(cont.)*

Using the Practice Pages

Practice pages provide instruction for each day of the school year. Teachers may wish to prepare packets of weekly practice pages for the classroom or for homework. As outlined on page 4, every page is aligned to phonics and word recognition skills.

The week starts with introductory activities. The focus for the first half of the week is to familiarize students with the words of the week.

Each day of the week focuses on a new skill. There are five overarching skills used in this book: introducing, recognizing, playing, using, and writing with the words. See page 7 for detailed objectives for each day.

Each week students explore new words through kinesthetic activities.

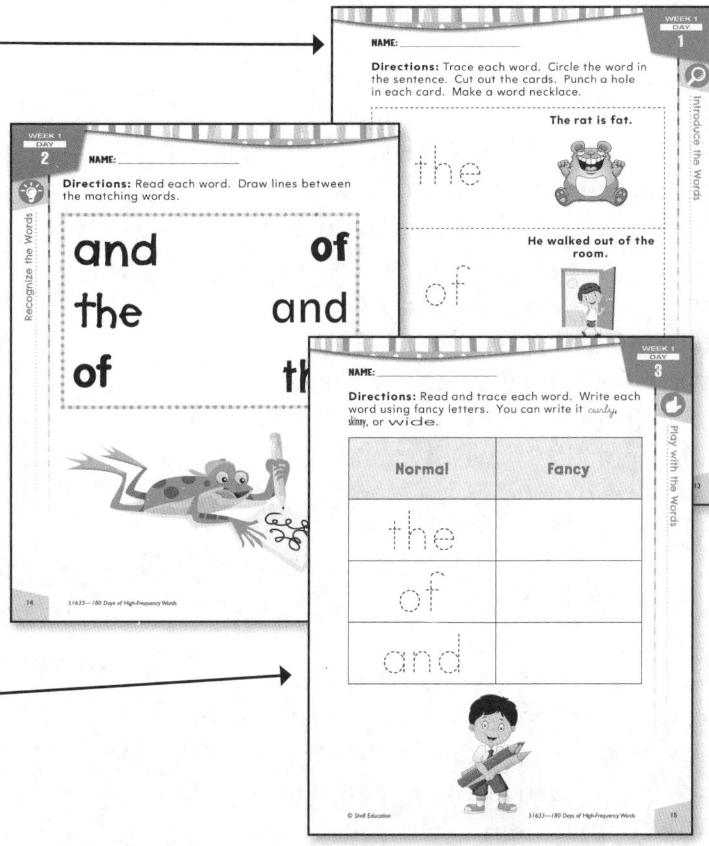

At the end of the week, students read and write using the high-frequency words of the week. For a detailed explanation of each activity, see pages 8–9.

HOW TO USE THIS BOOK *(cont.)*

Using the Resources

The student extension activities, assessment materials, and flash cards in this book are available as digital PDFs and Microsoft Word® documents online. A complete list of the available documents is provided on page 216. To access the Digital Resources, go to: www.tcmpub.com/download-files. Enter this code: 90507248. Follow the on-screen directions.

The quarterly assessment tools will aid the classroom teacher in tracking the high-frequency words your class recognizes throughout the year. The checklist on page 11 should be reproduced for each student in the class. Use it to record the words students recognize each quarter. Use page 12 to log students' progress throughout the year. This page can be used to see, at a glance, common high-frequency words that still need additional practice, as well as trends to drive whole-class instruction.

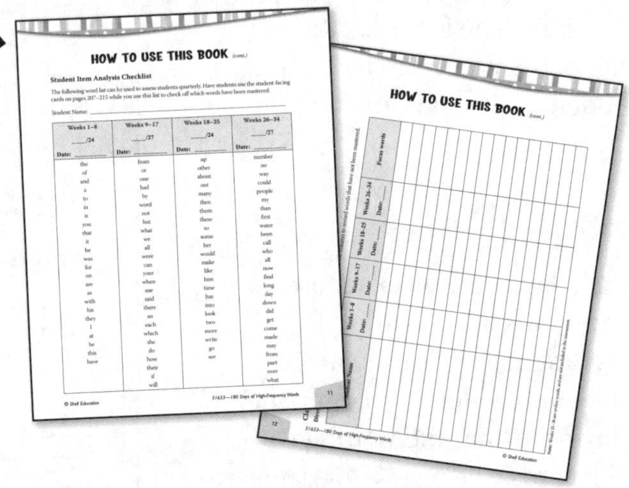
HOW TO USE THIS BOOK (cont.)

Student Item Analysis Checklist

HOW TO USE THIS BOOK (cont.)

Pages 199–206 can be used for home/school connection extension activities. The games and suggestions are engaging and will help students practice reading and identifying all of the high-frequency words in this book.

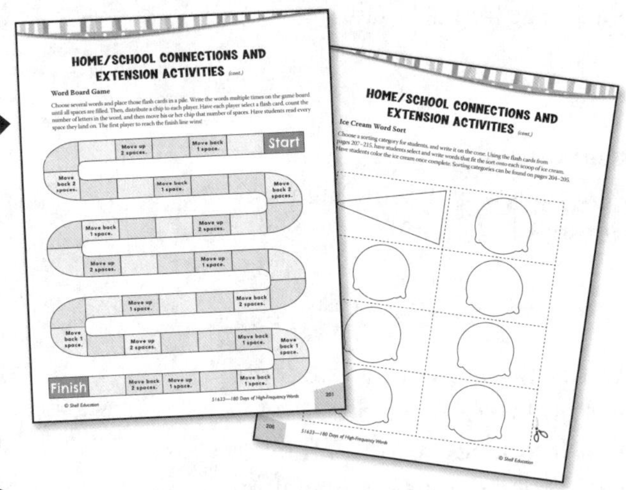
HOME/SCHOOL CONNECTIONS AND EXTENSION ACTIVITIES (cont.)

Word Board Game

Start

Finish

HOME/SCHOOL CONNECTIONS AND EXTENSION ACTIVITIES (cont.)

Ice Cream Word Sort

Dr. Edward Fry created a list of 1,000 Instant Words to teach children. That list was used in choosing the words for this series. On pages 207–215, the words from Fry's list that are used in this book are provided as flash cards. These cards can be used as a tool for the quarterly assessments. Additionally, these flash cards can be used with the home/school connection and extension activities.

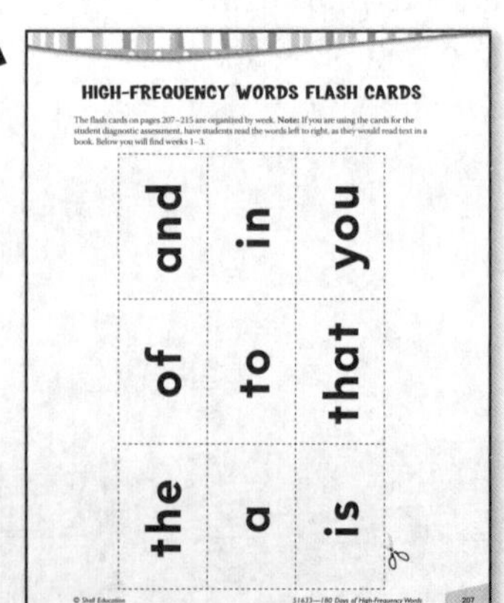
HIGH-FREQUENCY WORDS FLASH CARDS

the of and a to in is that you

HOW TO USE THIS BOOK *(cont.)*

For 180 days, teachers can use this book to support students' acquisition and recognition of high-frequency words. The book is divided into 36 weeks, with five days of activities per week. Each week, students are introduced to three high-frequency words. The format of the week is as follows: introduce the words, recognize the words, play with the words, use the words, and write the words.

Below is a list of daily activities. Detailed descriptions for each activity can be found on pages 8–9.

Daily Description	Names of Activities
Day 1—Introduce the Words For the first day of each week, students complete introductory activities. These activities are designed to introduce and familiarize students with the high-frequency words of the week. Students will create flash cards with the high-frequency words. These can be stored in a zip-top bag at each student's desk or taken home as a study tool for the week.	Letter Order Picture Words Word Books Word Find Word Necklace
Day 2—Recognize the Words The second day of each week is devoted to recognition activities. Activities are designed around identifying the high-frequency words of the week.	Hidden Words Letter Order Word Match Word Shapes
Day 3—Play with the Words On day three, students play with the words of the week. These activities are geared toward tactile manipulation of the high-frequency words. These activities infuse play, art, and hands-on activities for the week.	Color by Word Fancy Words Missing Letter Race to the Finish Scrambled Words Yarn Words
Day 4—Use the Words On the fourth day of the week, students use the words of the week in context. Students tell or write stories using the words, or act as word detectives and read the words.	Finish the Sentence Missing Letter Tell a Story Word Detective Word Locator
Day 5—Write the Words On day five, students engage in writing activities. Using the high-frequency words of the week, students craft stories and illustrations. These activities motivate all students to apply what they have learned during the week.	Sneaky Words Word Pictures Write and Draw

HOW TO USE THIS BOOK *(cont.)*

Below is a detailed explanation and rationale for each activity in *180 Days of High-Frequency Words for Kindergarten.*

Activity	Description
Color by Word	To complete this activity, the student will use a code to color in specific sections of a picture based on the high-frequency word printed in each area. For example, if the word *down* is assigned the color red, then the student will color every area red that contains the word *down*. The picture is complete when every section has been colored based on the code.
Fancy Words	After reading and tracing the words in the chart, students write the words themselves, using 'fancy' styles. Fancy styles might include using skinny, curly, or wide letters to write the words. Students can use the fonts modeled in the directions to complete this activity.
Finish the Sentence	Students start by locating the high-frequency word in each sentence and circling it. Next, they write their own words in the blank spaces to complete the sentences.
Hidden Words	At the beginning of the year, students search for each high-frequency word in lines of random letters, then circle the words once they find them. The activity becomes more challenging during the second half of the year. Students are asked to search for and circle each high-frequency word in three lines of random text. Each high-frequency word appears multiple times within the text.
Letter Order	Students begin by cutting out the individual letter squares. Next, they use the letter squares to form each high-frequency word and glue the letters in the correct order. After creating and gluing each word, students write the high-frequency words independently.
Missing Letter	For this activity, students fill in the letter missing from the high-frequency word in each sentence. Once the sentences are complete, they read the sentences and then draw pictures in the provided boxes.
Picture Words	Students begin by reading the words and examining the provided pictures. Next, they orally share sentences about the pictures for the words. For example, if the picture shows a beach scene and one of the high-frequency words is *have*, students might say, "Let's *have* a picnic at the beach." After creating their sentences, students write the words and color the pictures.
Race to the Finish	Students use game boards to practice the high-frequency words of the week. Students cut out and mix up the flash cards. Once selected, the student says each word and moves to that tile on the board until he or she reaches the finish line. Students can then work in pairs to practice racing to the finish on their own. When they run out of cards, have students reshuffle and reuse the deck.
Scrambled Words	Students complete this activity by unscrambling the letters to write high-frequency words.
Sneaky Words	For this activity, students draw pictures (they choose the subject matter) and then hide the high-frequency words within the pictures. The teacher should demonstrate how to hide the words by writing them in obscure locations within the picture, such as hidden within the leaves of a tree or on a person's T-shirt. The words should be difficult, but not impossible, to find.

HOW TO USE THIS BOOK *(cont.)*

Activity	Description
Tell a Story	Students start by reading the sentences and tracing the high-frequency words on the story cards. Next, students cut out the story cards and glue them in the correct sequential order on the boxes provided.
Word Books	In this activity, students create their own small books introducing each of the high-frequency words. They start by tracing each word and cutting along the dotted lines to make the pages of the book. Then, they staple the pages together to make books. Once their books are complete, they can use them to review the high-frequency words.
Word Detective	To complete this activity, students write the appropriate high-frequency words in the blank spaces in order to complete the sentences.
Word Find	Students begin this activity by reading each of the three sentences. Next, they circle the high-frequency words in the sentences and write them on the provided lines.
Word Locator	For this activity, students begin by cutting out the word cards containing the high-frequency words at the bottom of the page. After cutting out the words, they read each sentence and glue the appropriate high-frequency words into the blank spaces to complete the sentences.
Word Match	Students complete this activity by drawing lines between the matching high-frequency words in each column.
Word Necklace	Students begin this activity by tracing the high-frequency words and circling them in the sentences. Next, students cut out the cards and punch holes at the top of the cards. To complete their necklaces, students string the cards onto yarn and tie knots to finish their necklaces.
Word Pictures	In this activity, students trace the high-frequency words and then write them on the provided lines. After writing the words, they orally share sentences using at least one of the high-frequency words and draw pictures of their sentences in the provided boxes.
Word Shapes	In this activity, students use the shape of the high-frequency words to determine where to write them. Each shape box contains one box for each letter in the word. Tall letters have tall boxes (e.g., *l, k, t*); drop letters have long boxes (e.g., *j, g, q*); and small letters have square boxes (e.g., *o, s, e*). The students examine the shapes of the letters in the high-frequency words and then write the letters into the correct boxes in the word shapes to form the high-frequency words.
Write and Draw	In the first half of the year, students complete this activity by reading the provided sentences and writing words in the blank spaces to complete the sentences. After completing the sentences, they draw pictures relating to the text. In the second half of the year, students are challenged to independently write their own sentences, using at least one high-frequency word. Then, they draw pictures to go with their sentences.
Yarn Words	Students make high-frequency words out of yarn in this activity. First, they read the words, and then they form each letter using yarn. After students have the letters formed, they glue the yarn on top of the letters. It is also possible to use dried beans, small pom-pom balls, dried pasta, or other objects in place of yarn.

HOW TO USE THIS BOOK *(cont.)*

Diagnostic Quarterly Assessment

Teachers can use the *Student Item Analysis Checklist* to monitor students' learning. This tool can enable teachers or parents to quickly score students' work and monitor students' progress. Teachers and parents can see which high-frequency words students know and which ones they do not.

The words in this book are divided into four lists. Each list can be used to assess students quarterly throughout the year. The *Student Item Analysis Checklist* on page 11 should be used by the teacher to administer the assessment. The *High-Frequency Word Flash Cards* on pages 207–215 should be used as the student-facing list. Below you will find detailed steps to administer each component of the diagnostic assessment.

To Complete the Student Item Analysis Checklist:

- Write or type the student's name on the name line at the top of the chart. One copy per student is needed to track his or her ongoing progress throughout the year.
- Give each student the flash cards that correspond with the *Student Item Analysis Checklist* on page 11. Use the *Student Item Analysis Checklist* to mark students' responses. Students should be able to identify each word in a few seconds.
- The numbers across the top of the chart can be used to log each student's percentage of correct words in each quarter of the school year. For each quarter, record how many high-frequency words each student is able to accurately identify.

To Complete the Class Item Analysis:

- After each student has completed a list from the *Student Item Analysis Checklist,* use the *Class Item Analysis* chart on page 12 to log the results. Write or type students' names in the far-left column. Depending on the number of students in your class, more than one copy of the form may be needed, or you may need to add rows.
- Indicated across the top of the chart are the weeks that correspond with each word list. Students are assessed every 8 to 9 weeks. **Note:** Weeks 35 and 36 are review weeks and are therefore not included in the quarterly assessment chart.
- For each student, record his or her score in the appropriate column.
- Students' scores can be placed in the middle columns and scored by averaging the number of words in the week compared to the words identified correctly. Place the results in the correct column. Use these scores as benchmarks to determine how students are performing. This allows for four benchmark assessments during the year that can be used to gather formative diagnostic data. Use the last column to identify trends in the classroom for additional high-frequency lesson planning.

HOW TO USE THIS BOOK *(cont.)*

Student Item Analysis Checklist

The following word list can be used to assess students quarterly. Have students use the student-facing cards on pages 207–215 while you use this list to check off which words have been mastered.

Student Name: ______________________________

Weeks 1–8 _____/24 Date: ________	Weeks 9–17 _____/27 Date: ________	Weeks 18–25 _____/24 Date: ________	Weeks 26–34 _____/27 Date: ________
the	from	up	number
of	or	other	no
and	one	about	way
a	had	out	could
to	by	many	people
in	word	then	my
is	not	them	than
you	but	these	first
that	what	so	water
it	we	some	been
he	all	her	call
was	were	would	who
for	can	make	all
on	your	like	now
are	when	him	find
as	use	time	long
with	said	has	day
his	there	into	down
they	an	look	did
I	each	two	get
at	which	more	come
be	she	write	made
this	do	go	may
have	how	see	from
	their		part
	if		over
	will		what

Class Item Analysis

Directions: Record students' quarterly progress in the chart. Use the last column to record words that have not been mastered.

Student Name	Weeks 1–8 Date: ___	Weeks 9–17 Date: ___	Weeks 18–25 Date: ___	Weeks 26–34 Date: ___	Focus words

Note: Weeks 35–36 are review words, and are not included in the assessment.

NAME: ______________________________

Directions: Trace each word. Circle the word in the sentence. Cut out the cards. Punch a hole in each card. Make a word necklace.

The rat is fat.

the

He walked out of the room.

of

I see a dog and a pig.

and

NAME: ______________________

Directions: Read each word. Draw lines between the matching words.

and	of
the	and
of	the

NAME: ____________________

Directions: Read and trace each word. Write each word using fancy letters. You can write it curly, skinny, or wide.

Normal	Fancy
the	
of	
and	

NAME: ____________________

Use the Words

Directions: Cut apart the words. Glue them into the correct phrases. Read each phrase.

1. a boy ______________ a girl

2. lots ______________ candy

3. in ______________ car

of	the	and

NAME: ______________________

Directions: Read the words. Make up a sentence about the picture using all the words. Tell a friend your sentence. Write each word and color the picture.

the	of	and

NAME: ____________________

Introduce the Words

Directions: Draw a picture. Hide each word somewhere in your picture.

a	to	in

NAME: ______________________

Directions: Circle the correct spelling of the word. Trace over the word with your crayons.

1. a

an   a   aa

2. to

ti   tti   to

3. in

in   iin   ini

Play with the Words

NAME: ______________________

Directions: Read the words. Form each letter with yarn. Glue the yarn over the letters.

1. in

2. a

3. to

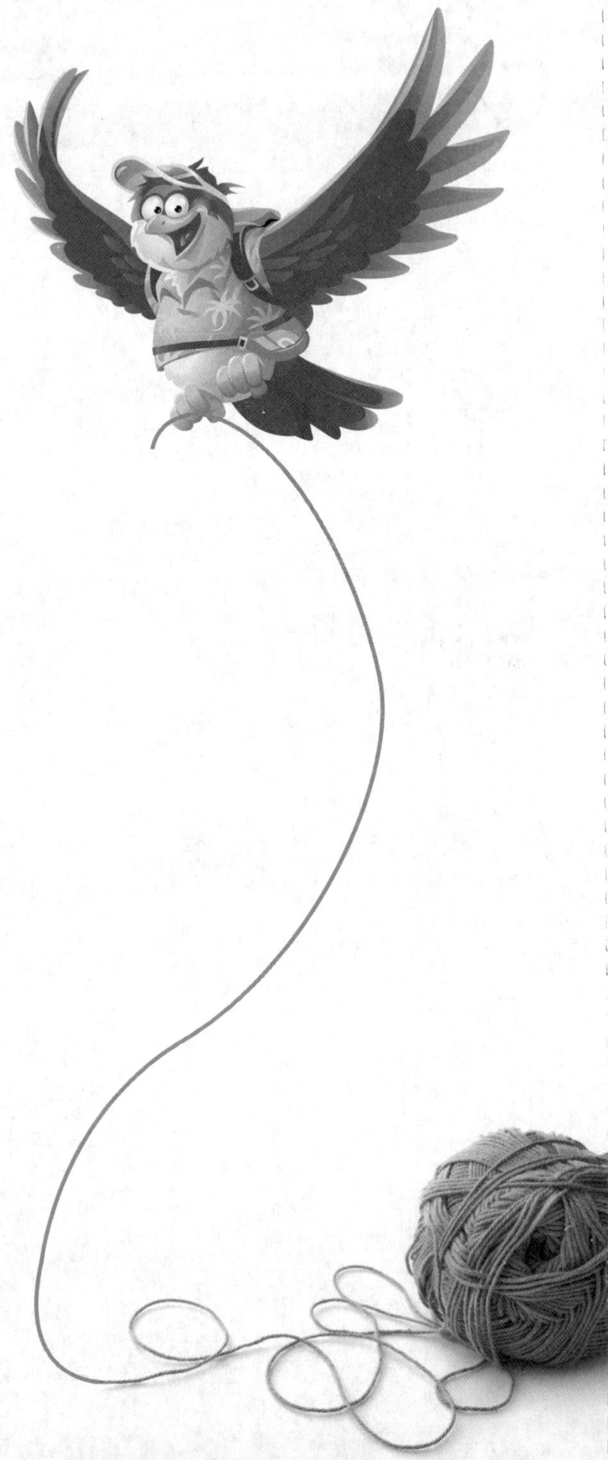

NAME: ______________________

Directions: Draw lines to put the story in order.

1

2

3

Put it in a pan.

in

Bake a cake!

a

Mix to make a cake.

to

Write the Words

NAME: ____________________

Directions: Finish the story using the words of the week. Draw a picture showing the story.

to	a	in

I see ____________ cake!

It is ____________ the store.

I want ____________ eat the cake.

NAME: ____________________

Directions: Trace each word. Cut along the lines. Staple the pages together. Read each word.

My Words Book **is** **you** **that**	is
you	that

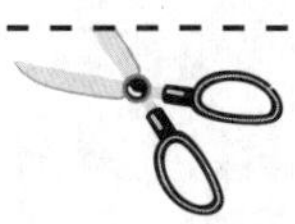

NAME: ____________________

Directions: Read each word. Find the hidden words. Circle the hidden words.

that	is	you

akeobthatmyons

uqoetpmxiciscjw

tyoqutyoumnoyu

NAME: ______________________________

Directions: Read the words. Use the color code to complete the picture.

you:	is:	that:
blue	red	black

Use the Words

NAME: ______________________

Directions: Fill in the missing letter. Read the sentence. Draw a picture for each sentence.

is	that	you

1. Can yo____ see me?

2. I like t____at hat!

3. My cat ____s black.

NAME: ____________________

Directions: Trace each word. Write each word twice. Then, draw each word in bubble letters.

1. you

2. that

3. is

NAME: ______________________

Directions: Trace each word. Circle the word in the sentence. Cut out the cards. Punch a hole in each card. Make a word necklace.

it

I see it.

he

He looks sad.

was

She was asleep.

NAME: ______________________

Directions: Read each word. Draw lines between the matching words.

was	it
it	he
he	was

NAME: ______________________

Play with the Words

Directions: Read and trace each word. Write each word using fancy letters. You can write it curly, skinny, or wide.

Normal	Fancy
he	
it	
was	

NAME: ______________________

Directions: Cut apart the words. Glue them into the correct phrases. Read each phrase.

1. He ____________________ hot.

2. Then, __________________ got a drink.

3. Yes, __________________ was good!

he	was	it

NAME: ____________________

Directions: Read the words. Make up a sentence about the picture using all the words. Tell a friend your sentence. Write each words and color the picture.

was	he	it

____________ ____________ ____________

NAME: ____________________

Directions: Draw a picture. Hide each word somewhere in your picture.

for	on	are

NAME: ______________________

Recognize the Words

Directions: Circle the correct spelling of the word. Trace over the word with your crayons.

1. on

on in un

2. are

aree ar are

3. for

fur forr for

NAME: ____________________

Directions: Read the words. Form each letter with yarn. Glue the yarn over the letters.

Play with the Words

1. on

2. for

3. are

NAME: ______________________________

Use the Words

Directions: Draw lines to put the story in order.

1	**We put it on her pillow.** on 
2	**We are writing a letter.** are 
3	**It is for our mom.** for 

NAME: ______________________

Directions: Finish the story using the words of the week. Draw a picture showing the story.

on	for	are

We got a gift ____________ mom. We put it ____________ her pillow. We ____________ happy.

NAME: ______________________________

Directions: Trace each word. Cut along the lines. Staple the pages together. Read each word.

My Words Book **as** **with** **his**	as
with	his

NAME: ______________________

Directions: Read each word. Find the hidden words. Circle the hidden words.

his	with	as

iuwthizewithypwih

apaasthaqapusniw

hmtyucplehjishisxs

NAME: ______________________

Directions: Read the words. Use the color code to complete the picture.

his:	**as:**	**with:**
brown	**black**	**pink**

NAME: ______________________

Directions: Fill in the missing letter. Read the sentence. Draw a picture for each sentence.

as	with	his

1. I am a______ tall as my mom.

2. I see ______is fish.

3. Can I go w______th you?

Write the Words

NAME: ______________________

Directions: Trace each word. Write each word twice. Then, draw each word in bubble letters.

Example: big big

1. as

2. with

3. his

NAME: ____________________________

Directions: Trace each word. Circle the word in the sentence. Cut out the cards. Punch a hole in each card. Make a word necklace.

they

They are happy.

I

I like you.

at

He is at home.

NAME: ______________________

Directions: Read each word. Draw lines between the matching words.

at	I
I	they
they	at

NAME: ____________________________

Directions: Read and trace each word. Write each word using fancy letters. You can write it curly, skinny, or wide.

Normal	Fancy
I	
at	
they	

NAME: ______________________

Use the Words

Directions: Cut apart the words. Glue them into the correct phrases. Read each phrase.

1. ______________________ school

2. ______________________ run

3. ______________________ swim

they	at	I

NAME: ______________________________

Directions: Draw a picture. Hide each word somewhere in your picture.

I	at	they

Introduce the Words

NAME: ____________________

Directions: Read the words. Make up a sentence about the picture using all the words. Tell a friend your sentence. Write the words and color the picture.

be	this	have

NAME: ______________________________

Directions: Circle the correct spelling of the word. Trace over the word with your crayons.

1. this

this thes tis

2. be

bea bi be

3. have

hav have

hove

NAME: ____________________

Directions: Read the words. Form each letter with yarn. Glue the yarn over the letters.

1. have

2. be

3. this

NAME: ____________________

Directions: Draw lines to put the story in order.

1

2

3

I can stand on this.

this

I have a box.

have

I want to be tall!

be

NAME: ____________________

Write the Words

Directions: Finish the story using the words of the week. Draw a picture showing the story.

have	this	be

I ____________ a pen. ____________ will help me write. I want to ____________ an author.

NAME: ______________________

Directions: Trace each word. Cut along the lines. Staple the pages together. Read each word.

My Words Book **from** **or** **one**	from
or	one

Recognize the Words

NAME: ______________________

Directions: Read each word. Find the hidden words. Circle the hidden words.

one	from	or

upztyoneiypwonve

urthpuornuuyokfet

houclehjisfromisus

NAME: ______________________

Directions: Read the words. Use the color code to complete the picture.

from:	or:	one:
green	yellow	blue

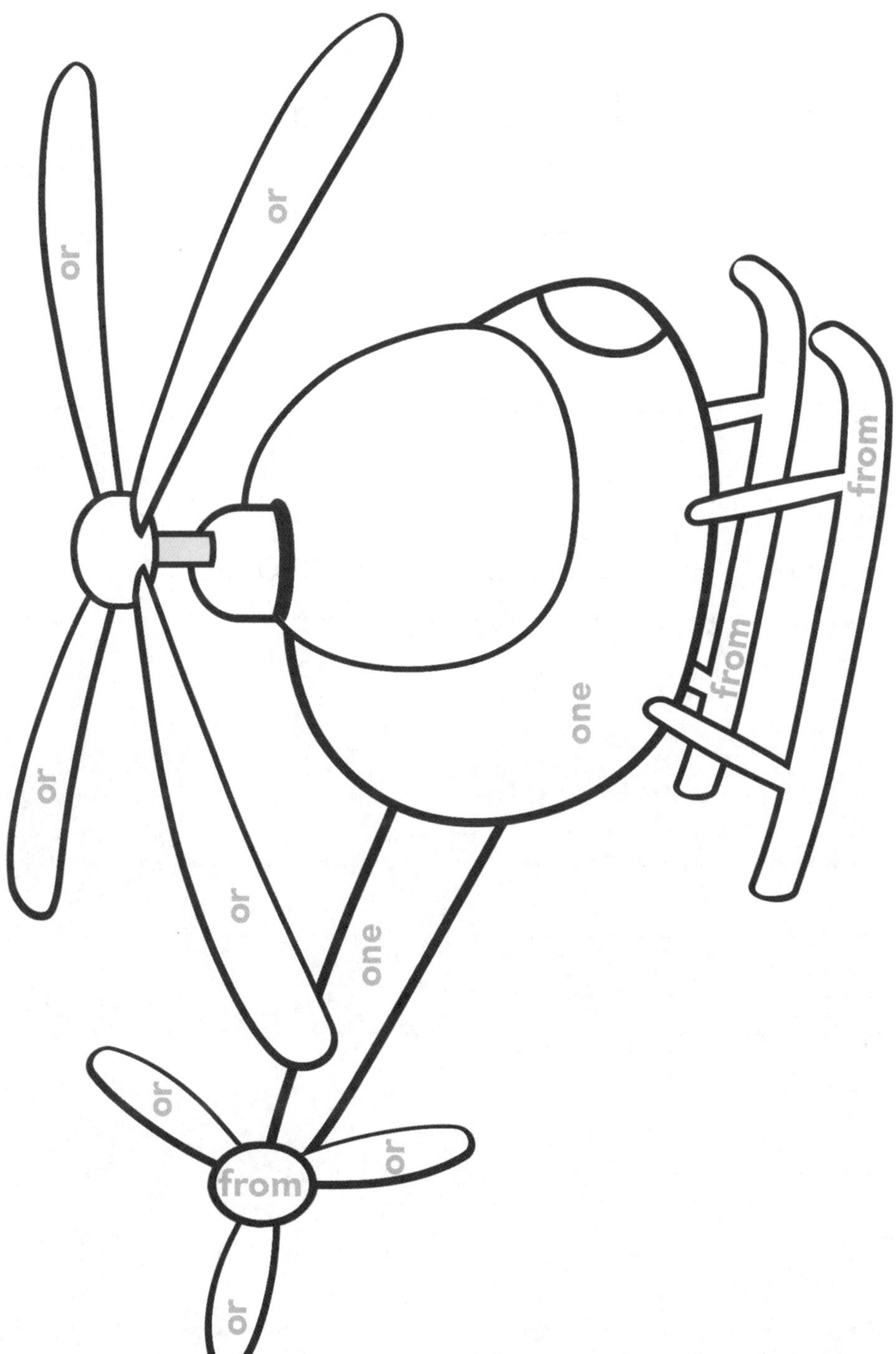

NAME: ____________________

Directions: Fill in the missing letter. Read the sentence. Draw a picture for each sentence.

one	from	or

1. I got a letter f_____om Pam.

2. The cake had o_____e candle.

3. Is it a cat o_____ a dog?

NAME: ____________________

Directions: Trace each word. Write each word twice. Then, draw each word in bubble letters.

Example: big big

1. or

2. one

3. from

NAME: ______________________

Introduce the Words

Directions: Trace each word. Circle the word in the sentence. Cut out the cards. Punch a hole in each card. Make a word necklace.

I had a good day.

had

Sit by me.

by

I like this word.

word

NAME: ______________________________

Directions: Read each word. Draw lines between the matching words.

by	by
had	word
word	had

NAME: ______________________________

Directions: Read and trace each word. Write each word using fancy letters. You can write it curly, skinny, or wide.

Normal	Fancy
had	
word	
by	

NAME: ______________________

Directions: Cut apart the words. Glue them into the correct phrases. Read each phrase.

1. a ______________________

2. ______________________ Sam

3. ______________________ fun

word	by	had

NAME: ______________________

Directions: Read each word. Write a sentence about the picture using each word. Color the picture.

by	work	had

NAME: ______________________

Directions: Draw a picture. Hide each word somewhere in your picture.

but	not	what

NAME: ____________________

Recognize the Words

Directions: Circle the correct spelling of the word. Trace over the word with your crayons.

1. not

nut noot not

2. but

but bot bit

3. what

wat whut

what

NAME: ______________________________

Directions: Read each word. Form each letter with yarn. Glue the yarn over the letters.

1. what

2. but

3. not

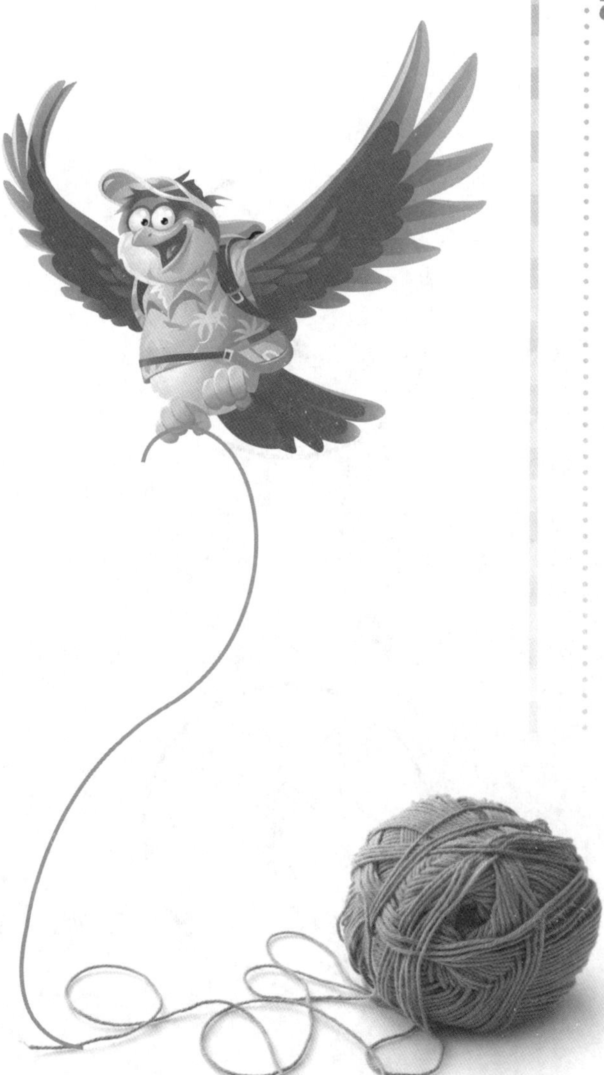

NAME: ____________________

Use the Words

Directions: Draw lines to put the story in order.

1

2

3

But it is still fun!

but

It is not a ball.

not

What is it?

what

NAME: ______________________

Directions: Finish the story using the words of the week. Draw a picture showing the story.

what	not	but

He asked, "______________ is this?" This is ____________ a bike. ____________ it is still fun!

NAME: ______________________

Introduce the Words

Directions: Trace each word. Cut along the lines. Staple the pages together. Read each word.

My Words Book **all** **were** **we**	all
were	we

NAME: ______________________

Directions: Read each word. Find the hidden words. Circle the hidden words.

we	all	were

tpekwajwurbhswe

ksthekslbllaluallleu

wtiwereksuwerksn

NAME: ______________________________

Directions: Read the words. Use the color code to complete the picture.

were:	we:	all:
green	brown	yellow

NAME: ______________________

Directions: Fill in the missing letter. Read the sentence. Draw a picture for each sentence.

all	were	we

1. W____ love you.

2. I see a____l the pets.

3. We____e you sad?

Write the Words

NAME: ______________________

Directions: Trace the word, then write each word. Write a sentence using some of the words. Draw a picture of your sentence.

1. all

2. we

3. were

NAME: ______________________

Directions: Trace each word. Circle the word in the sentence. Cut out the cards. Punch a hole in each card. Make a word necklace.

When can you play?

when

I like your hat.

your

Can you see me?

can

Recognize the Words

NAME: ______________________

Directions: Read each word. Draw lines between the matching words.

can	when
your	your
when	can

NAME: ______________________________

Directions: Read and trace each word. Write each word using fancy letters. You can write it **curly**, skinny, or wide.

Normal	Fancy
your	
when	
can	

Use the Words

NAME: ____________________

Directions: Cut apart the words. Glue them into the correct sentence. Read each sentence.

1. I ____________________ skip.

2. ____________________ is Monday?

3. ____________________ mom waves.

when	can	your

NAME: ______________________

Directions: Read the words. Make up a sentence about the picture using all the words. Tell a friend your sentence. Write each words and color the picture.

can	when	your

NAME: ____________________

Directions: Draw a picture. Hide each word somewhere in your picture.

said	there	use

NAME: ______________________

Directions: Circle the correct spelling of the word. Trace over the word with your crayons.

1. use

use usu uss

2. said

said sad

siad

3. there

the ther

there

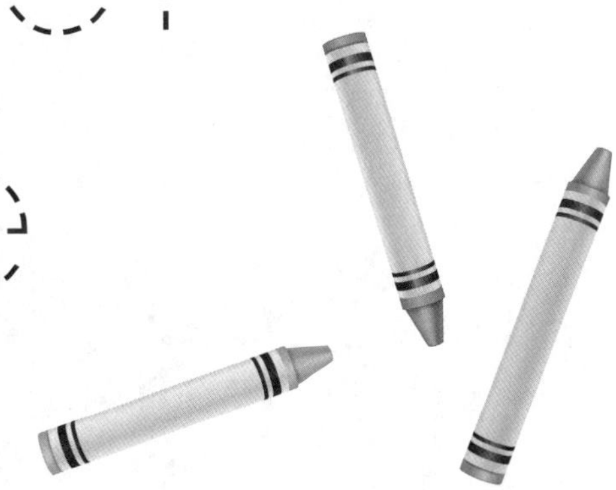

Play with the Words

NAME: ____________________

Directions: Read the words. Form each letter with yarn. Glue the yarn over the letters.

1. said

2. there

3. use

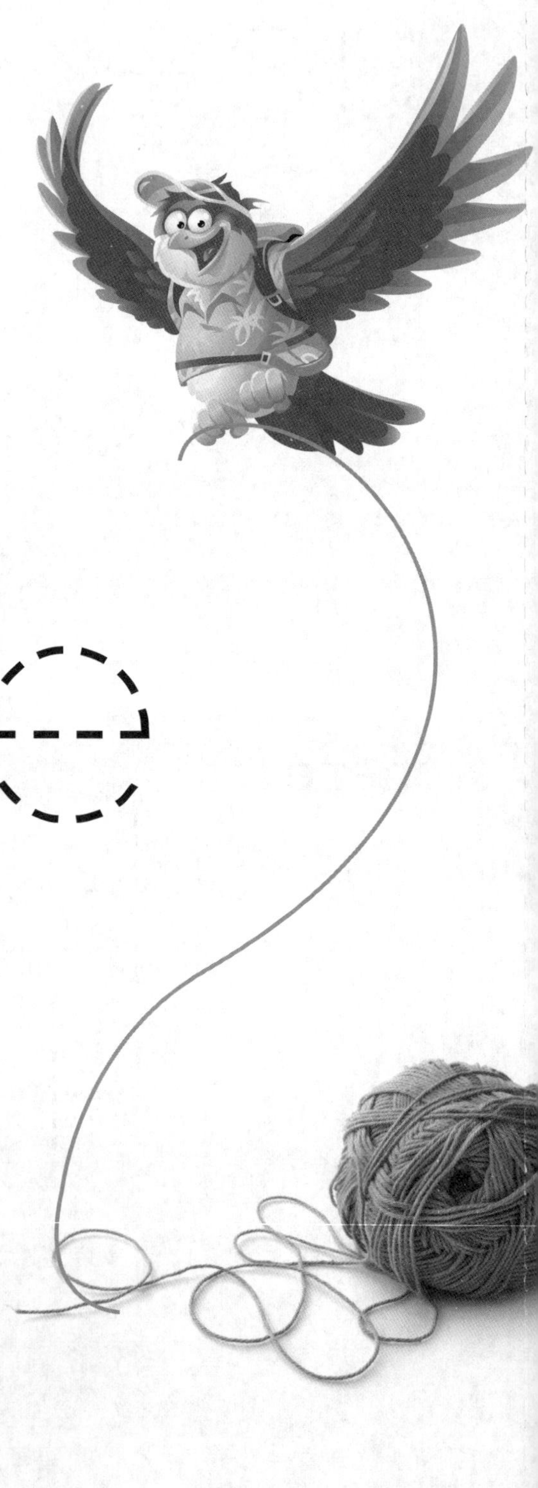

NAME: ______________________

Directions: Draw lines to put the story in order.

1

2

3

Let's use this.

use

There is a hole.

there

I said, "We have to fix it!"

said

Write the Words

NAME: ______________________

Directions: Finish the story using the words of the week. Draw a picture showing the story.

use	There	said

She ____________, "____________ is a ball!

Let's ____________ it to play."

NAME: ______________________________

Directions: Trace each word. Cut along the lines. Staple the pages together. Read each word.

My Words Book **an** **each** **which**	an
each	which

Recognize the Words

NAME: ____________________

Directions: Read each word. Find the hidden words. Circle the hidden words.

which	an	each

wichilbmqwhichs

skeianslxcisamoii

siejblelkeachksuw

NAME: ______________________________

Directions: Read each word. Use the color code to complete the picture.

each:	which:	an:
purple	yellow	green

NAME: ______________________

Use the Words

Directions: Fill in the missing letter. Read the sentence. Draw a picture for each sentence.

each	an	which

1. Here is ____n apple.

2. E____ch kid has a ball.

3. Wh____ch one do you like?

NAME: ______________________

Directions: Trace the word, and write each word. Create a sentence using some of the words. Draw a picture of your sentence.

1. which ______________________
2. an ______________________
3. each ______________________

____

____

NAME: ______________________

Directions: Trace each word. Circle the word in the sentence. Cut out the cards. Punch a hole in each card. Make a word necklace.

She did it!

she

Do you want to try?

do

Show me how to draw.

how

NAME: ______________________

Directions: Read each word. Draw lines between the matching words.

she	do
do	she
how	how

NAME: ____________________

Directions: Read and trace each word. Write each word using fancy letters. You can write it **curly**, skinny, or wide.

Normal	Fancy
she	
how	
do	

NAME: ____________________

Directions: Cut apart the words. Glue them into the correct sentence. Read each sentence.

1. I can ______________ my work.

2. Can ______________ see you?

3. Look ______________ fast it goes!

do	she	how

Write the Words

NAME: ____________________

Directions: Draw a picture. Hide each word somewhere in your picture.

how	she	do

NAME: ____________________

Directions: Read the words. Make up a sentence about the picture using all the words. Tell a friend your sentence. Write each words and color the picture.

their	if	will

____________ ____________ ____________

NAME: ______________________

Recognize the Words

Directions: Circle the correct spelling of the word. Trace over the word with your crayons.

1. if

ik uf if

2. their

their ther

thir

3. will

wil wall will

NAME: ______________________

Directions: Read the words. Form each letter with yarn. Glue the yarn over the letters.

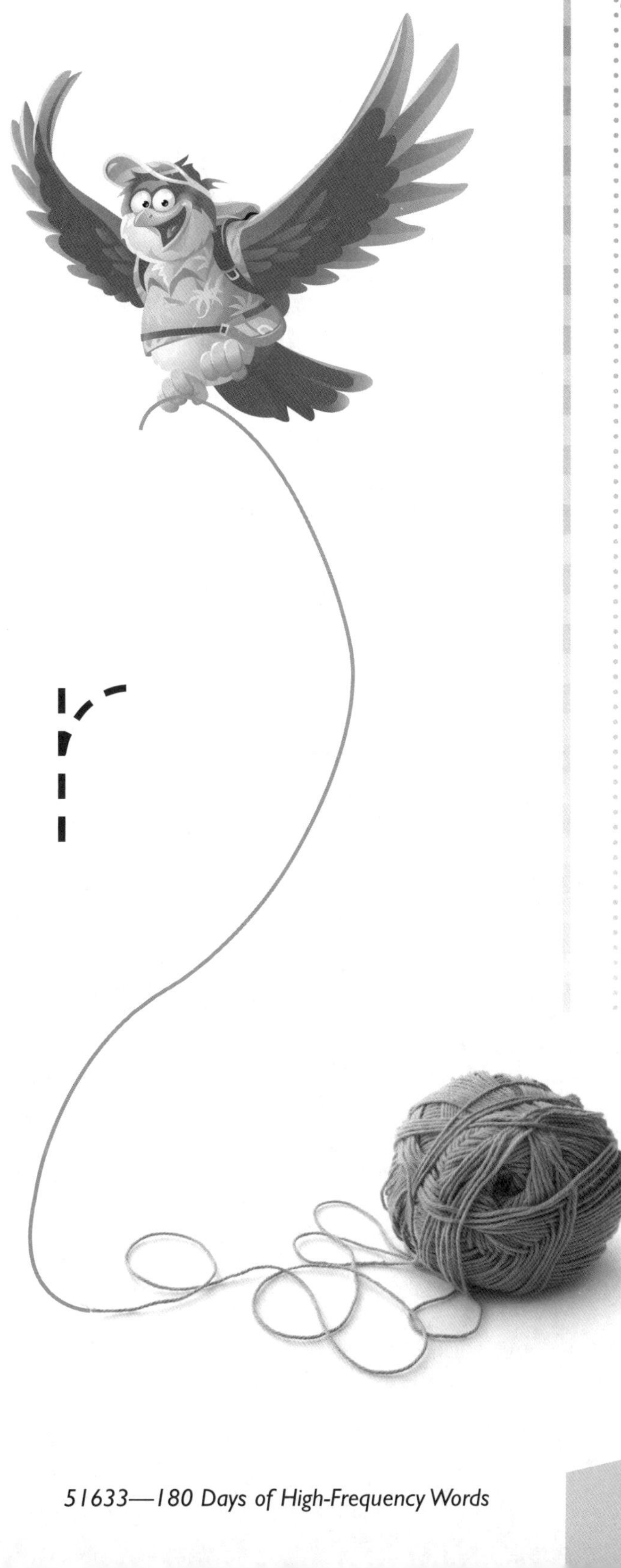

1. will

2. their

3. if

Use the Words

NAME: ______________________

Directions: Draw lines to put the story in order.

1

2

3

We will use a leash!

will

What if it runs away?

if

Their dog wants to go out.

their

NAME: ______________________

Directions: Finish the story using the words of the week. Draw a picture showing the story.

their	if	will

What ______________ they name ______________ dog?

I would name it Jax ______________ I could.

NAME: ____________________

Directions: Trace each word. Cut along the lines. Staple the pages together. Read each word.

My Words Book **up** **other** **about**	up
other	about

NAME: ____________________

Directions: Read each word. Find the hidden words. Circle the hidden words.

about	up	other

k s i a b o u t k s h j o u t

s i k e k a w u j s p u p l

s o i e o t h e r k d n o t r e

Play with the Words

NAME: ______________________

Directions: Read the words. Use the color code to complete the picture.

about:	up:	other:
green	yellow	black

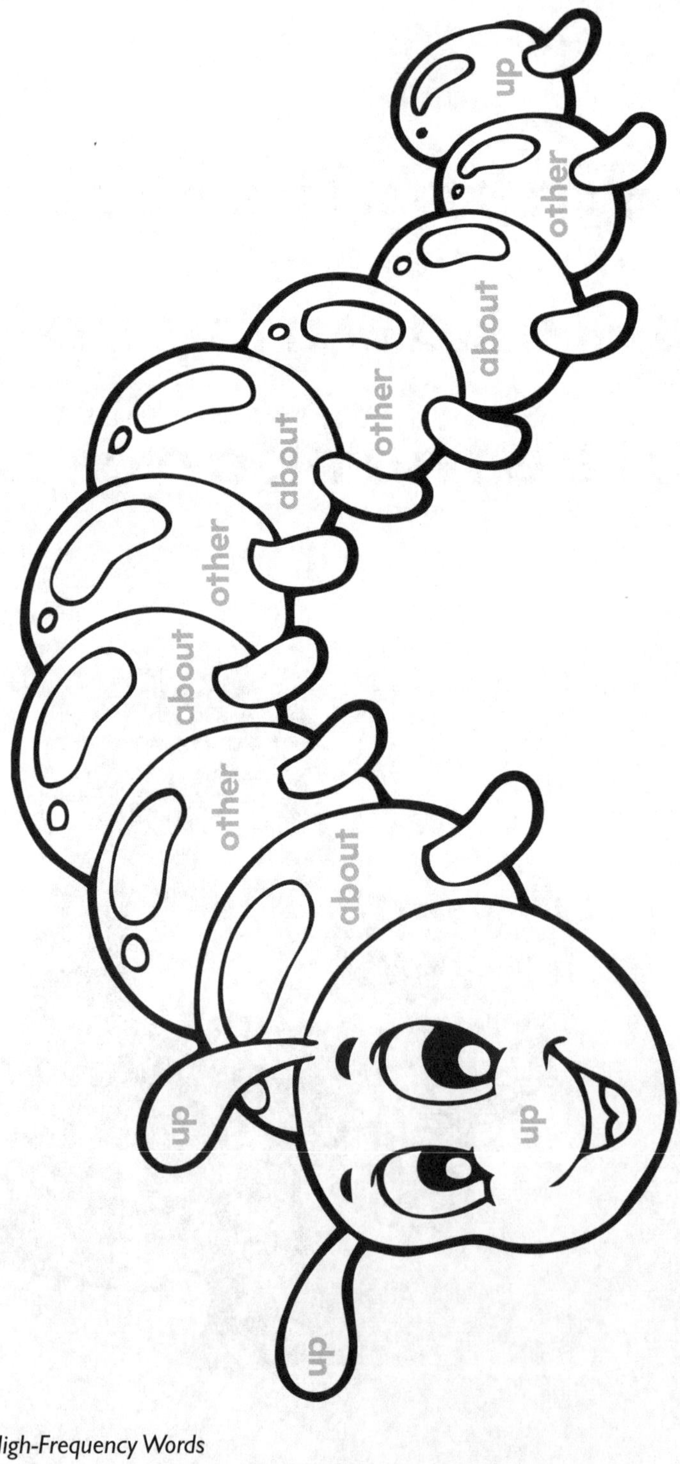

NAME: ____________________

Directions: Fill in the missing letter. Read the sentence. Draw a picture for each sentence.

up	other	about

1. The rat is ____p on top.

2. What ab____ut me?

3. Do you see the oth____r kids?

Write the Words

NAME: ____________________

Directions: Trace each word. Write each word twice. Create a sentence using some of the words. Draw a picture of your sentence.

1. other
2. up
3. about

NAME: ____________________

Directions: Read the sentences. Circle the words of the week in each sentence. Write each word three times.

out	many	then

Many kids were playing. ____________________

The girl went out. ____________________

Then, the boy went down. ____________________

NAME: ______________________

Directions: Read each word. Draw lines between the matching words.

many	out
out	many
then	then

NAME: ______________________________

Directions: Read and trace each word. Write each word using fancy letters. You can write it curly, skinny, or wide.

Normal	Fancy
many	
out	
then	

NAME: ______________________

Directions: Cut apart the words. Glue them into the correct phrases. Read each phrase.

1. Look ____________________!

2. I have ________________ pets.

3. ____________________, I will go home.

then	many	out

Write the Words

NAME: ______________________

Directions: Write about the picture shown. Make sure to use at least two of the words.

out	many	then

NAME: ____________________

Directions: Trace each word. Circle the word in the sentence. Cut out the cards. Punch a hole in each card. Make a word necklace.

I see them.

them

These are my friends.

these

The cake is so good!

so

NAME: ____________________

Directions: Look at the shape of the word. Find the box with that shape. Write each letter in a box.

these   them   so

Example: g i r l

1.

2.

3.

Recognize the Words

NAME: ____________________

Directions: Read the words. Form each letter with yarn. Glue the yarn over the letters.

1. so

2. them

3. these

Use the Words

NAME: ______________________

Directions: Fill in the missing letter. Read the sentence. Draw a picture for each sentence.

these	so	them

1. Th_____se bags are big.

2. Can you see th_____m?

3. The sun is _____o hot!

Write the Words

NAME: ____________________

Directions: Write a sentence. Use at least one word. Draw a picture of your sentence.

them	so	these

NAME: ____________________

Directions: Cut out the letters. Make each word. Glue the letters in order. Write each word.

some

her

would

d	h
l	e
u	s
r	o
o	e
w	m

NAME: ____________________

Directions: Circle the correct spelling of the word. Trace over the word with your crayons.

1. would

wold woud

would

2. some

sume some

soo

3. her

her har

here

NAME: ______________________

Directions: Unscramble the letters to write each word three times.

some	would	her

1. lwuod

2. reh

3. meso

NAME: ______________________

Use the Words

Directions: Draw lines to put the story in order.

first

second

third

I have some cupcakes.

some

Give one to her, too!

her

Would you like one?

would

Write the Words

NAME: ____________________

Directions: Trace each word. Write each word twice. Create a sentence using some of the words. Draw a picture of your sentence.

1. some
2. would
3. her

NAME: ______________________

Directions: Read each word. Write a sentence about the picture using each word. Tell a friend your sentence. Color the picture.

make	like	him

NAME: ____________________

Directions: Read each word. Find the hidden words. Circle the hidden words.

him	like	make

s k e k l h i m h s i x o a k m e i s

h i k s h e h n m k s h e l i k e s l

k h m i l s k m a k e i s h l q n g

Play with the Words

NAME: ______________________________

Directions: Read each word. Use the color code to complete the picture.

make:	him:	like:
orange	yellow	green

NAME: ______________________

Directions: Cut apart the words. Glue them into the correct phrases. Read each phrase.

1. I sat with ____________________ .

2. We ____________________ ice cream.

3. Let's ____________________ a snowman!

like	him	make

Write the Words

NAME: ____________________

Directions: Draw a picture. Hide each word somewhere in your picture. Write each word three times.

him	like	make

NAME: ____________________

Directions: Trace each word. Cut along the lines. Staple the pages together. Read each word.

My Words Book **into** **time** **has**	has
time	into

NAME: ____________________

Recognize the Words

Directions: Look at the shape of the word. Find the box with that shape. Write each letter in a box.

time	has	into

Example: b o y

1.

2.

3.

NAME: ______________________________

Directions: Cut out the game cards at the bottom. Each partner picks a card and moves to that word. Play until you both reach the finish line.

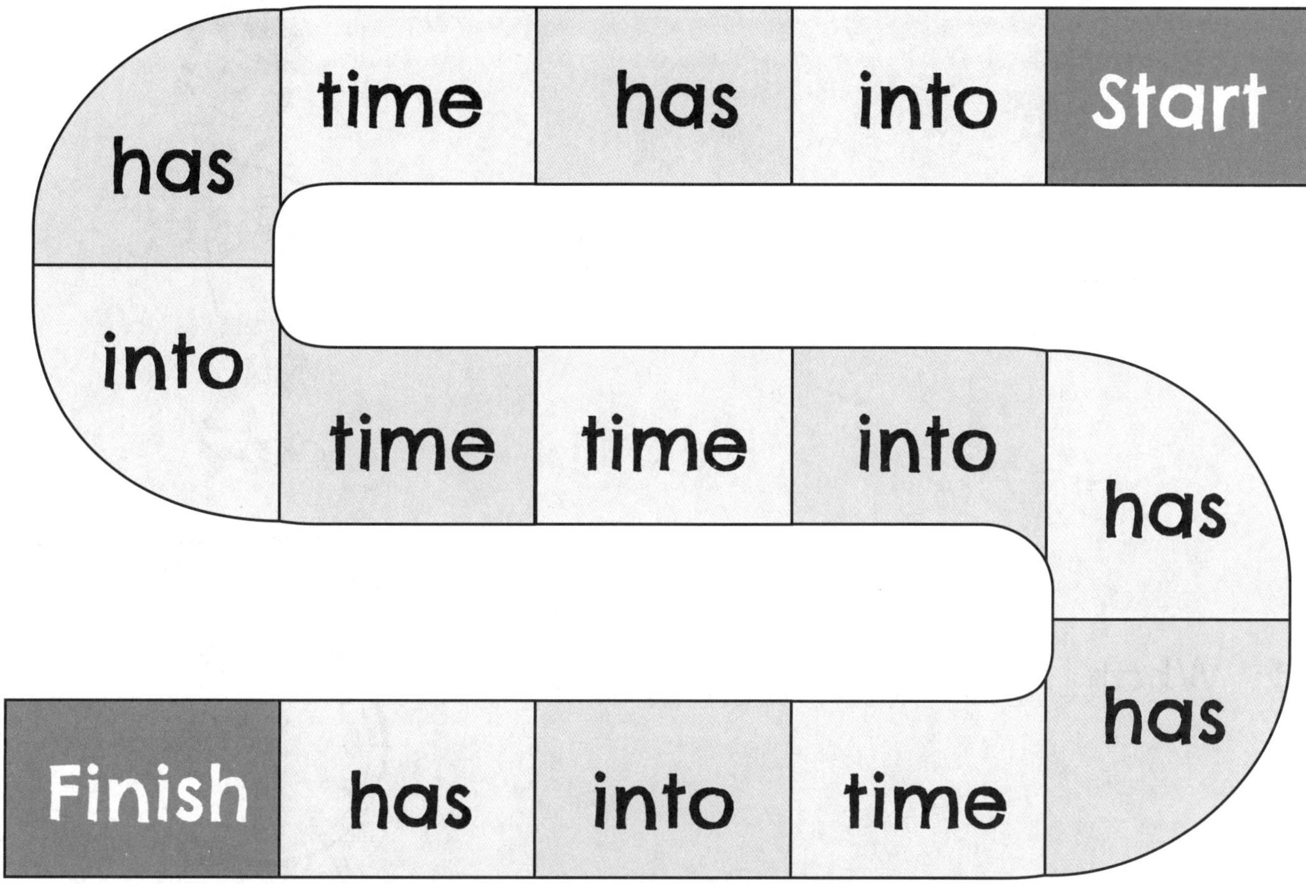

time	time	time	time
into	into	into	into
has	has	has	has

Use the Words

NAME: ____________________________

Directions: Cut apart the words. Glue them into the correct sentence. Read each sentence.

1. He ____________________ a fish.

2. What ____________________ is it?

3. Go ____________________ the house.

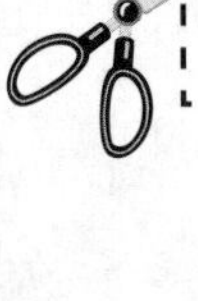

time	into	has

NAME: ______________________

Directions: Write a sentence. Use at least one word. Draw a picture of your sentence.

has	into	time

WEEK 24
DAY
1

Introduce the Words

NAME: ______________________________

Directions: Trace each word. Circle the word in the sentence. Cut out the cards. Punch a hole in each card. Make a word necklace.

Look at the snow!

look

I have two hands.

two

Can I have more milk?

more

NAME: ____________________

Directions: Read each word. Draw lines between the matching words.

look	two
two	more
more	look

NAME: ______________________

Play with the Words

Directions: Unscramble the letters to write each word three times.

look	more	two

1. roem ______________________

2. otw ______________________

3. olok ______________________

NAME: ____________________

Directions: Write in each missing word.

look	more	two

1. I have one ____________ candy left.

2. The cat has ____________ kittens.

3. ____________ at the rainbow!

NAME: ____________________

Directions: Read the words. Make up a sentence about the picture using all the words. Tell a friend your sentence. Write the sentence and color the picture.

look	more	two

NAME: ______________________

Directions: Cut out the letters. Make each word. Glue the letters in order. Write each word.

write

go

see

e	o
e	e
g	t
s	i
r	w

NAME: ______________________

Directions: Circle the correct spelling of the word. Trace over the word with your crayons.

1. see

sei see se

2. write

write wriite

writ

3. go

goo gu go

NAME: ______________________

Directions: Read and trace each word. Write each word using fancy letters. You can write it curly, skinny, or wide.

Normal	Fancy
write	
see	
go	

NAME: ____________________

Use the Words

Directions: Fill in each missing word.

go	see	write

1. I can ____________ my name.

2. Let's ____________ to the park.

3. I ____________ my mom.

NAME: ______________________

Directions: Trace each word. Write each word twice. Then, draw each word in bubble letters.

Example: big big

1. see

2. go

3. write

NAME: ______________________

Directions: Read the sentences. Circle the words of the week in each sentence. Write each word three times.

number	no	way

This is house number one. ______________

No one is home. ______________

Let's go this way! ______________

NAME: ______________________

Directions: Read each word. Find each hidden word twice. Circle the hidden words.

no	number	way

disnoskenlkswyaois

kshenumberlsksoke

skdjwaylkzumborks

WEEK 26
DAY
3

Play with the Words

NAME: ______________________________

Directions: Read the words. Use the color code to complete the picture.

way:	no:	number:
red	black	yellow

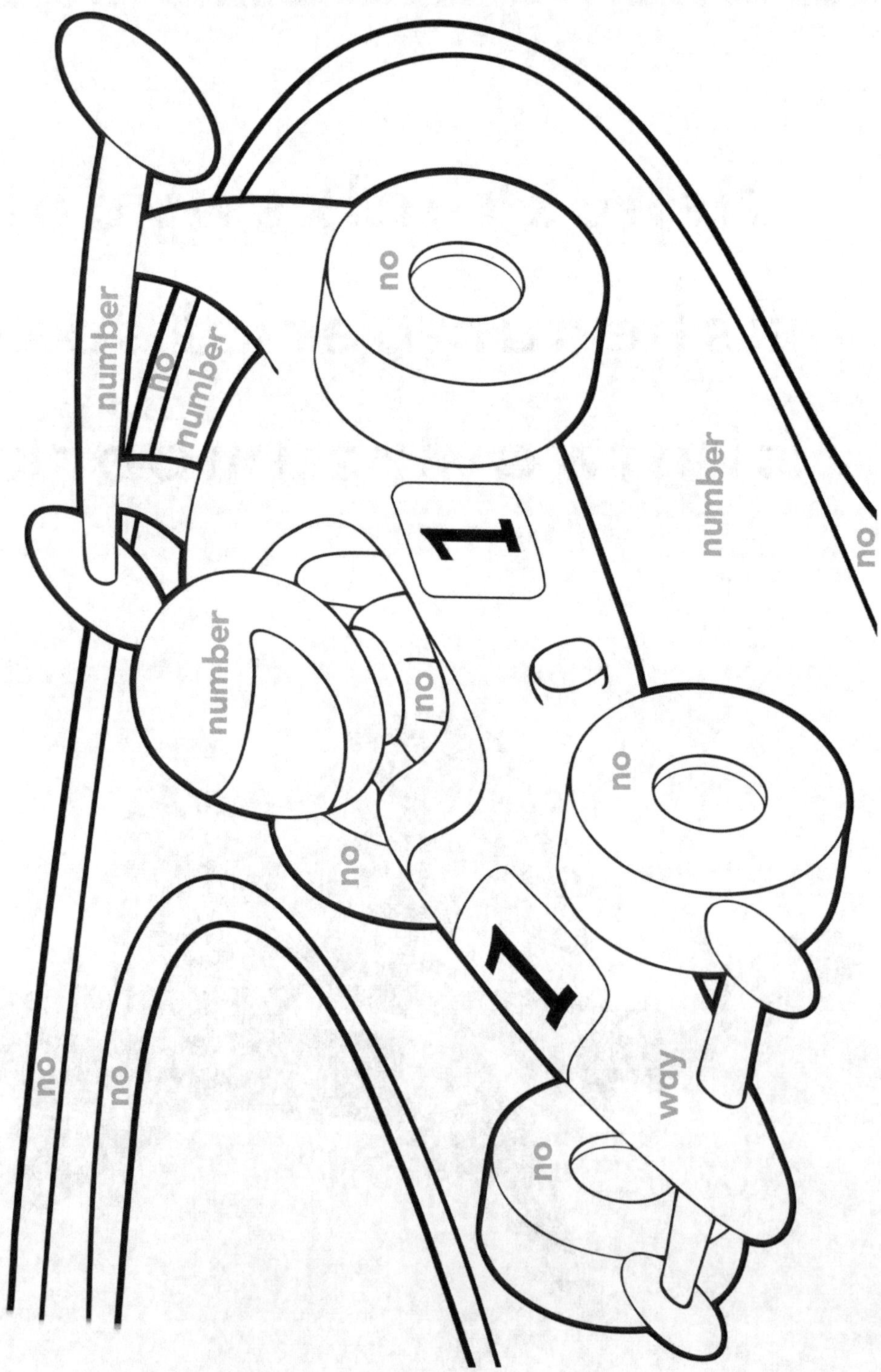

NAME: ______________________

Directions: Draw lines to put the story in order.

first

second

third

No one can find him.

no

Count to number ten.

number

This way!

way

Write the Words

NAME: ____________________

Directions: Write a sentence. Use at least one word. Draw a picture of your sentence.

way	number	no

NAME: ______________________

Directions: Trace each word. Cut along the lines. Staple the pages together. Read each word.

My Words Book **could** **people** **my**	could
people	my

NAME: ____________________

Recognize the Words

Directions: Look at the shape of the word. Find the box with that shape. Write each letter in a box.

people	could	my

Example: c a t

1.

2.

3.

NAME: ____________________

Directions: Read the words. Form each letter with yarn. Glue the yarn over the letters.

1. my

2. could

3. people

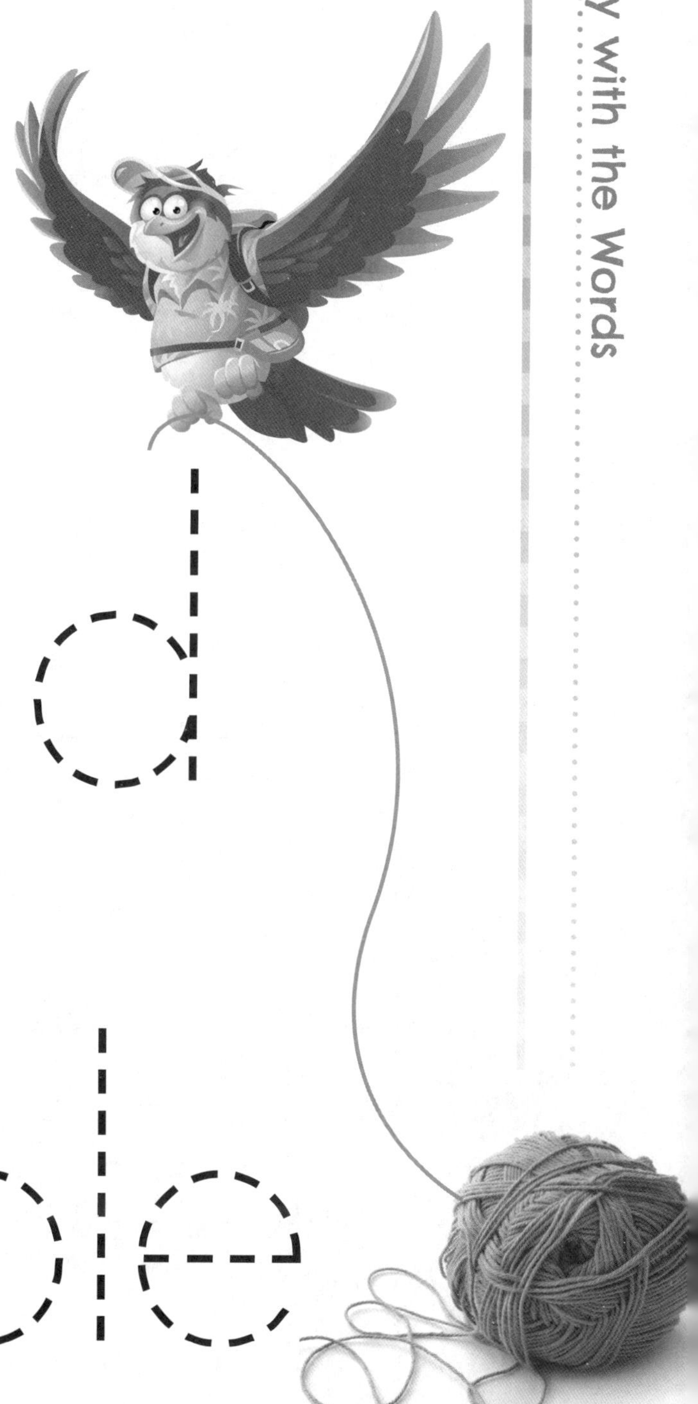

Use the Words

NAME: ______________________

Directions: Fill in the missing letter. Read the sentence. Draw a picture for each sentence.

could	My	people

1. ____y cat is black.

2. The peo____le are tall.

3. Cou____d you see me?

NAME: ______________________________

Directions: Write a sentence. Use at least one word. Draw a picture of your sentence.

could	my	people

NAME: ______________________

Directions: Read the words. Make up a sentence about the picture using all the words. Tell a friend your sentence. Write the sentence and color the picture.

than	first	water

NAME: ____________________

Directions: Circle the correct spelling of the word. Trace over the word with your crayons.

1. water

water woter
wate

2. than

then thaan
than

3. first

furst fist
first

NAME: ______________________________

Directions: Cut out the game cards at the bottom. Each partner picks a card and moves to that word. Play until you both reach the finish line.

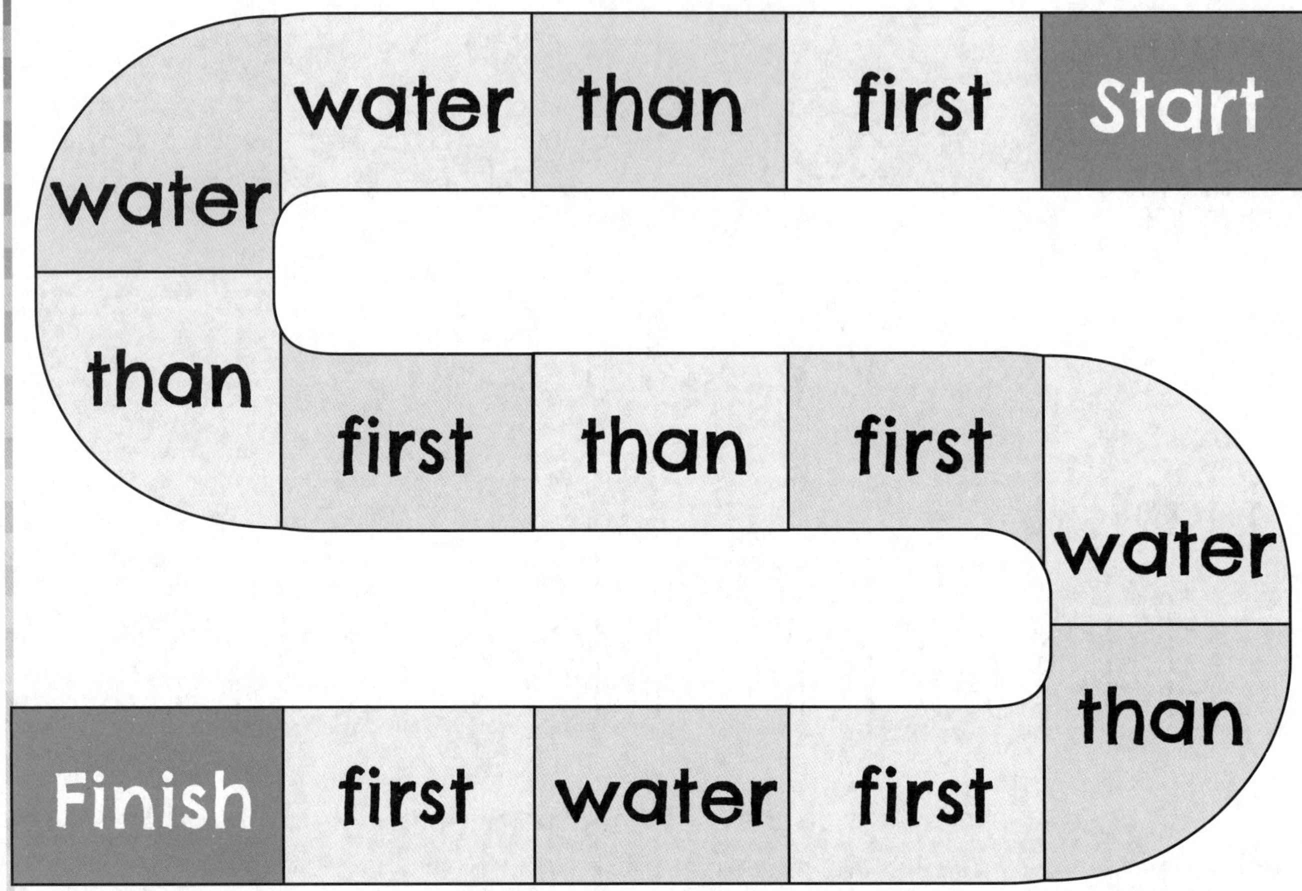

first	first	first	first
than	than	than	than
water	water	water	water

NAME: ____________________

Directions: Write in a word to complete the sentence.

than	water	first

1. The ____________ is very cold.

2. I won ____________ place in the race.

3 I am taller ____________ my brother.

NAME: ______________________

Write the Words

Directions: Trace each word. Write each word twice. Create a sentence using one of the words. Draw a picture of your sentence.

1. water

2. first

3. than

NAME: ____________________

Directions: Cut out the letters. Make each word. Glue the letters in order. Write each word.

been

____

call

____

who

____

o	c
n	h
a	e
w	l
e	l
b	

NAME: ____________________

Directions: Read each word. Find each hidden word twice. Circle the hidden words.

who	been	call

sifwhoksubeensi

skducallsiehwho

ksbeenskgucallx

NAME: ____________________________

Directions: Read and trace each word. Write each word using fancy letters. You can write it **curly**, skinny, or wide.

Normal	Fancy
who	
call	
been	

NAME: ______________________

Directions: Cut apart the words. Glue them into the correct sentence. Read each sentence.

1. ______________ is Jose?

2. He is making a ______________ .

3. It has ______________ raining.

call	been	Who

NAME: ______________________

Directions: Write about the picture shown. Make sure to use at least two of the words.

call	been	who

NAME: ____________________

Directions: Read the sentences. Circle the words of the week in each sentence. Write each word three times.

find	all	now

We can all look for it.

We can't find it.

Now I see it!

NAME: ____________________

Directions: Look at the shape of the word. Find the box with that shape. Write each letter in a box.

find	all	now

Example: w o r d

1.

2.

3.

Play with the Words

NAME: ______________________

Directions: Unscramble the letters to write each word three times.

all	now	find

1. lal ______________________
2. difn ______________________
3. own ______________________

NAME: ____________________

Directions: Fill in the missing letter. Read the sentence. Draw a picture for each sentence.

find	all	now

1. I love a____l of my family.

2. I can't f____nd my hat!

3. I want to go n____w.

NAME: ______________________________

Directions: Write a sentence. Use at least one word. Draw a picture of your sentence.

find	now	all

NAME: ____________________

Directions: Trace each word. Cut along the lines. Staple the pages together. Read each word.

My Words Book **long** **down** **day**	long
down	day

NAME: ______________________

Directions: Read each word. Draw lines between the matching words.

long	day
day	long
down	down

NAME: ______________________

Directions: Read each word. Use the color code to complete the picture.

day:	long:	down:
brown	green	red

NAME: ______________________

Directions: Fill in each missing word.

long	day	down

1. It is a hot ____________.

2. Go ____________ the slide

3. My hair is ____________.

NAME: ____________________

Directions: Write a sentence. Use at least one word. Draw a picture of your sentence.

down	day	long

NAME: ______________________

Introduce the Words

Directions: Write about the picture shown. Make sure to use at least two of the words.

did	get	come

NAME: ____________________

Directions: Read each word. Find each hidden word twice. Circle the hidden words.

get	come	did

dkdidksogetkskdi

comekshkdgetlske

kskcxdidscomeksb

Play with the Words

NAME: ____________________

Directions: Cut out the game cards at the bottom. Each partner picks a card and moves to that word. Play until you both reach the finish line.

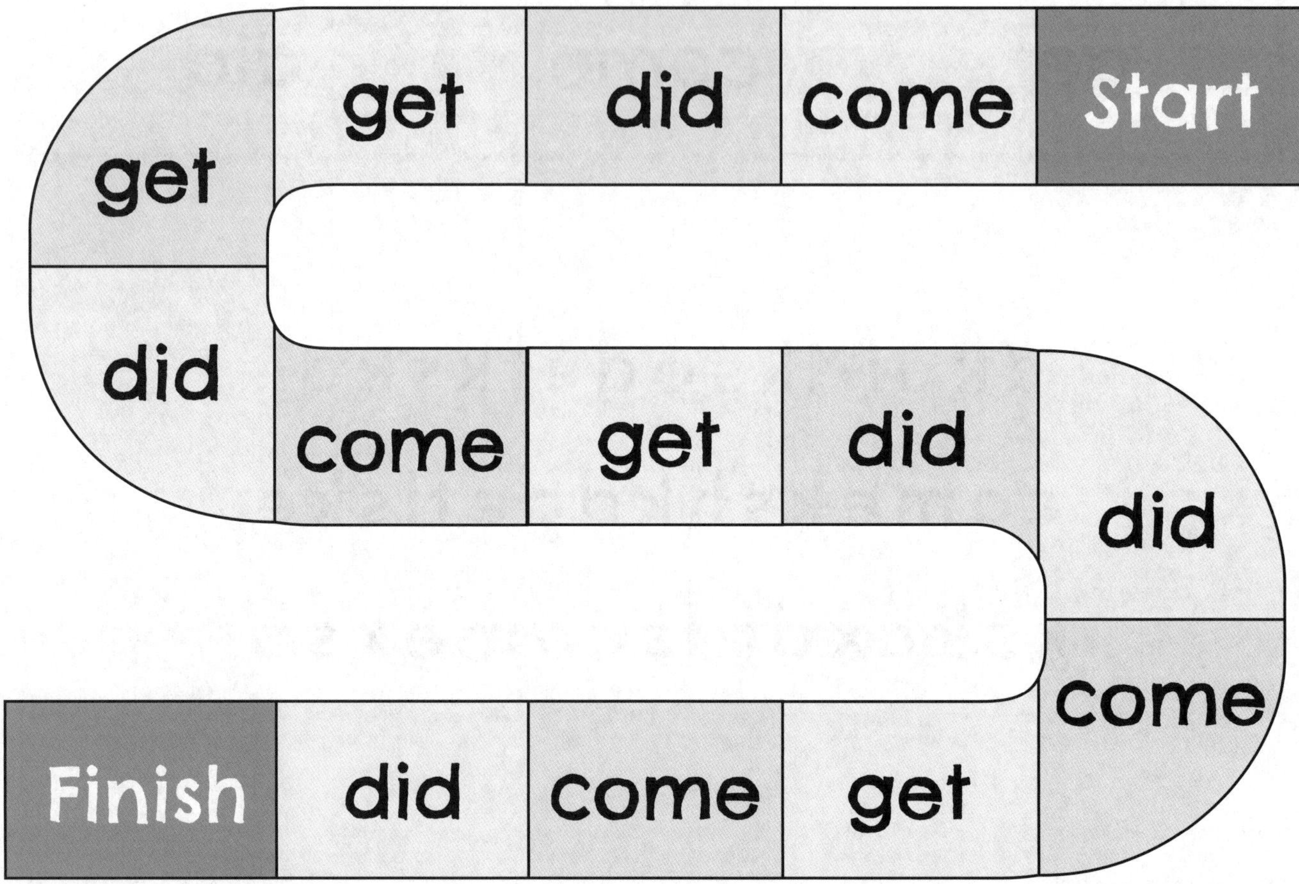

come	come	come	come
get	get	get	get
did	did	did	did

NAME: ______________________

Directions: Draw lines to put the story in order.

first

second

third

Did you have fun?

did

Let's get wet!

get

Come to the beach.

come

NAME: ______________________

Write the Words

Directions: Write about the picture shown. Make sure to use at least two of the words.

did	get	come

NAME: ____________________

Directions: Read the sentences. Circle the words of the week in each sentence. Write each word three times.

may	made	from

This vase is made of glass.

It is from my grandma.

May I hold it?

NAME: ______________________

Directions: Circle the correct spelling of the word. Trace over the word with your crayons.

1. may

mey maay

may

2. from

from frum

frome

3. made

mad mede

made

Play with the Words

NAME: ____________________

Directions: Unscramble the letters to write each word twice.

from	may	made

1. yma ____________________ ____________________

2. dame ____________________ ____________________

3. mfor ____________________ ____________________

NAME: ______________________

Use the Words

Directions: Write in a word to complete the sentence.

from	May	made

1. My dad picks me up ____________ school.

2. We ____________ posters today.

3. ____________ I have more food?

NAME: ______________________

Directions: Trace the word, then write each word. Create a sentence using some of the words. Draw a picture of your sentence.

1. may
2. from
3. made

Introduce the Words

NAME: ______________________

Directions: Cut out the letters. Make each word. Glue the letters in order. Write each word.

part

____

over

____

what

____

t	p
a	a
h	r
r	v
o	t
e	w

NAME: ____________________

Directions: Look at the shape of the word. Find the box with that shape. Write each letter in a box.

part	what	over

Example: b a n k

1.

2.

3.

NAME: ____________________

Directions: Read each word. Form each letter with yarn. Glue the yarn over the letters.

1. what

2. over

3. part

Use the Words

NAME: ____________________

Directions: Cut apart the words. Glue them into the correct sentence. Read each sentence.

1. Which ____________________ do you want?

2. Her hand is ____________________ my hand.

3. Do you know ____________________ time it is?

part	what	over

Write the Words

NAME: ____________________

Directions: Write a sentence. Use at least one word. Draw a picture of your sentence.

what	over	part

NAME: ______________________________

Directions: Trace each word. Circle the words in the sentence. Cut out the cards. Punch a hole in each card. Make a word necklace.

They are happy.

they

are

I have a bird.

I

have

He was on a bike.

was

a

Recognize the Words

NAME: ______________________

Directions: Read each word. Find each hidden word twice. Circle the hidden words.

many	be	said

isaidkbekshmanyx

ksudlbmanyskben

kslgjskbeupsaidlsv

NAME: ______________________________

Directions: Cut out the game cards at the bottom. Each partner picks a card and moves to that word. Play until you both reach the finish line.

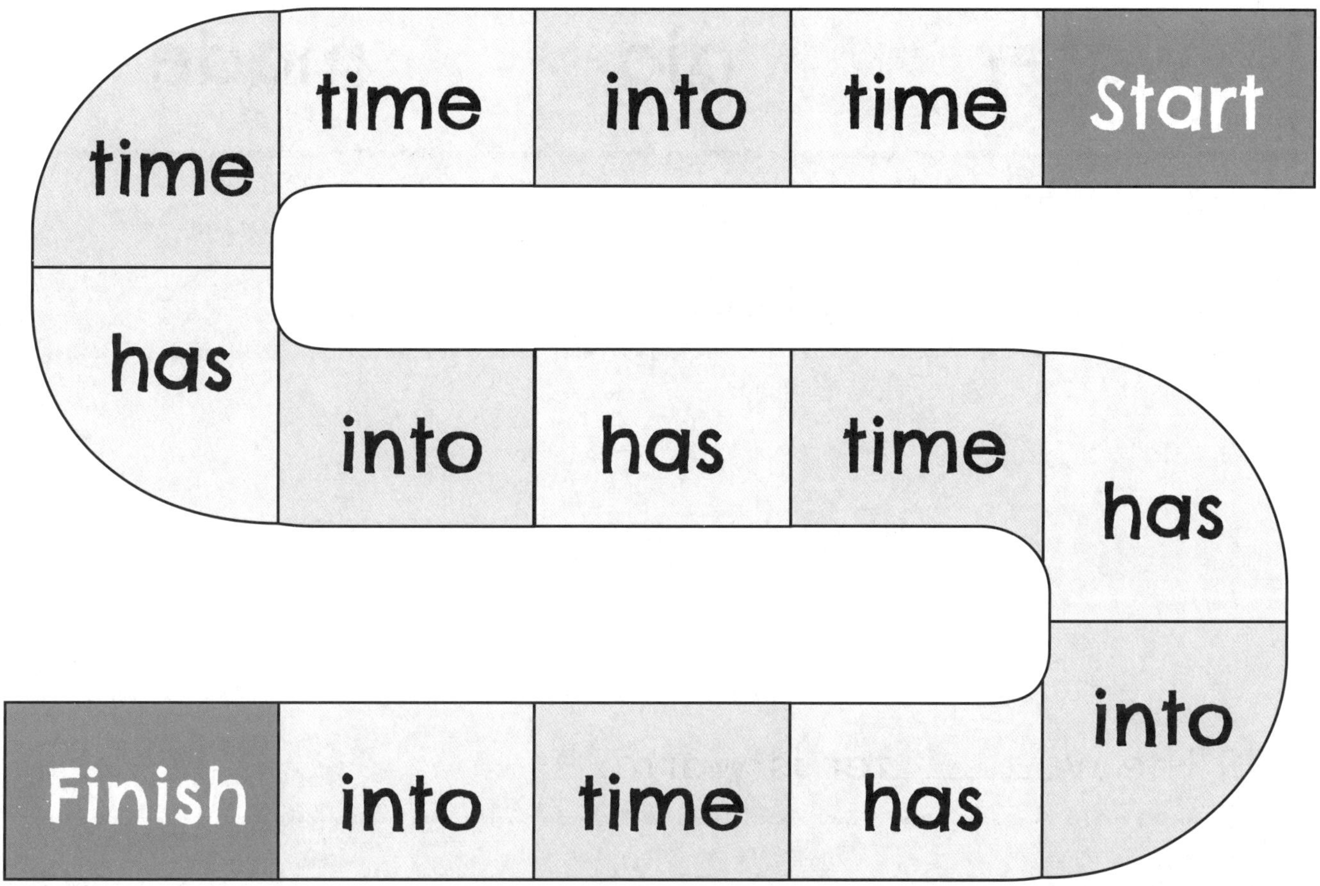

time	time	time	time
into	into	into	into
has	has	has	has

Use the Words

NAME: ____________________

Directions: Fill in the missing letter. Read the sentence. Draw a picture for each sentence.

water	did	made

1. I ma____e my bed.

2. The w____ter is warm.

3. My dog di____ it!

NAME: ______________________

Directions: Write a sentence. Use at least one word. Draw a picture of your sentence.

she	these	use

Introduce the Words

NAME: ______________________

Directions: Write about the picture shown. Make sure to use at least two of the words.

been	people	make

NAME: ____________________

Directions: Read each word. Draw lines between the matching words.

other	look
look	would
would	other

NAME: ______________________________

Play with the Words

Directions: Read and trace each word. Write each word using fancy letters. You can write it **curly**, skinny, or wide.

Normal	Fancy
who	
find	
more	

NAME: ____________________

Directions: Fill in each missing word.

about	their	were

1. ____________ shoes were wet.

2. We ____________ skating.

3. I am ____________ to go to bed.

Write the Words

NAME: ____________________

Directions: Write a sentence. Use at least one word. Draw a picture of your sentence.

could	my	people

ANSWER KEY

The activity pages that do not have specific answers to them are not included in this answer key. Students' answers will vary on these activity pages, so check that students are staying on task.

Week 1: Day 2 (page 14)

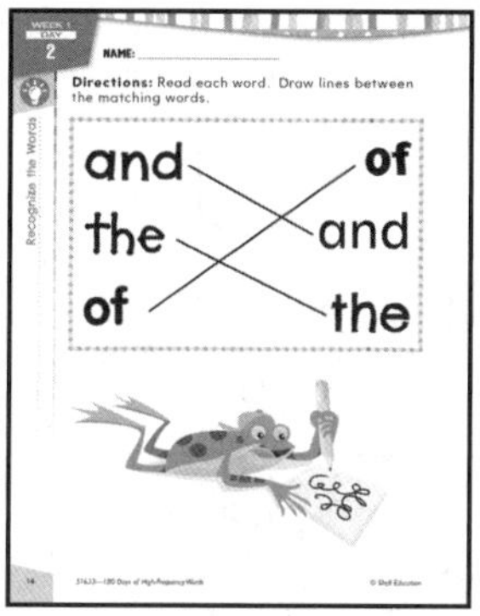

Week 1: Day 4 (page 16)

1. a boy **and** a girl
2. lots **of** candy
3. in **the** car

Week 2: Day 2 (page 19)

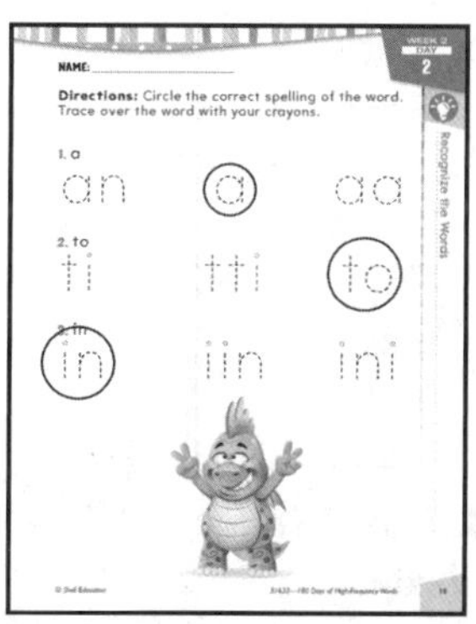

Week 2: Day 4 (page 21)

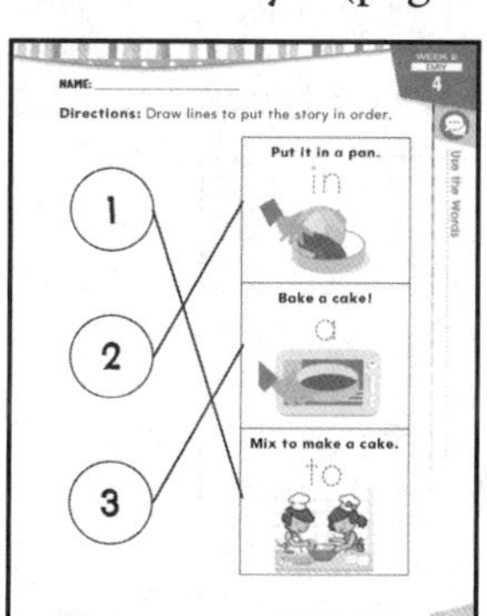

Week 2: Day 5 (page 22)

I see a cake.
It is in the store.
I want to eat the cake.

Week 3: Day 2 (page 24)

Week 3: Day 4 (page 26)

1. Can yo**u** see me?
2. I like t**h**at hat!
3. My cat **i**s black.

Week 4: Day 2 (page 29)

Week 4: Day 4 (page 31)

1. He **was** hot.
2. Then, **he** got a drink.
3. Yes, **it** was good!

Week 5: Day 2 (page 34)

Week 5: Day 4 (page 36)

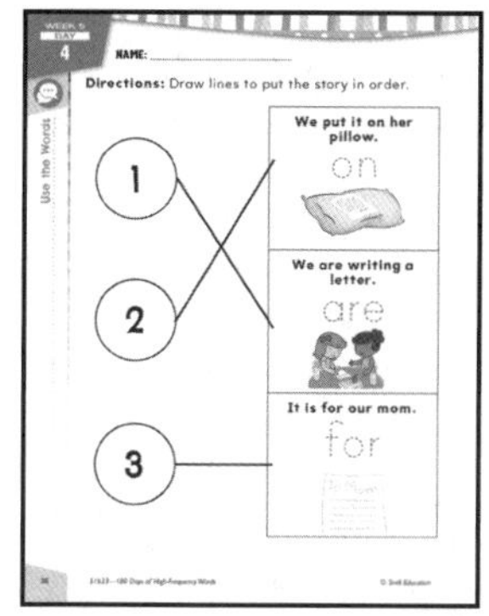

Week 5: Day 5 (page 37)

We got a gift for mom. We put it on her pillow. We are happy.

Week 6: Day 2 (page 39)

Week 6: Day 4 (page 41)

1. I am a**s** tall as my mom.
2. I see **h**is fish.
3. Can I go w**i**th you?

Week 7: Day 2 (page 44)

ANSWER KEY *(cont.)*

Week 7: Day 4 (page 46)

1. **at** school
2. **I** run
3. **They** swim

Week 8: Day 2 (page 49)

NAME:

Directions: Circle the correct spelling of the word. Trace over the word with your crayons.

1. this
this thes tis

2. be
bea bi be

3. have
hav have hove

Week 8: Day 4 (page 51)

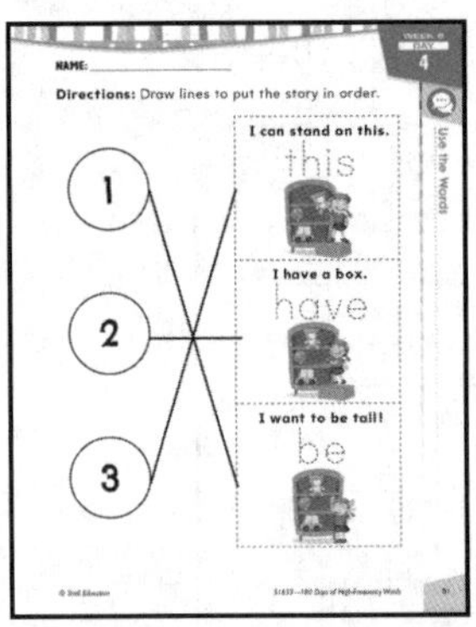
NAME:

Directions: Draw lines to put the story in order.

1 2 3

I can stand on this.
this

I have a box.
have

I want to be tall!
be

Week 8: Day 5 (page 52)

I <u>have</u> a pen. <u>This</u> will help me write I want to <u>be</u> an author.

Week 9: Day 2 (page 54)

NAME:

Directions: Read each word. Find the hidden word. Circle the hidden word.

one or from

upztyoneiypwonve
urthpuornuuyokfet
houclehjisfromisus

Week 9: Day 4 (page 56)

1. I got a letter **from** Pam.
2. The cake had **one** candle.
3. Is it a cat **or** a dog?

Week 10: Day 2 (page 59)

NAME:

Directions: Read each word. Draw lines between the matching words.

by — by
had — had
word — word

Week 10: Day 4 (page 61)

1. a **word**
2. **by** Sam
3. **had** fun

Week 11: Day 2 (page 64)

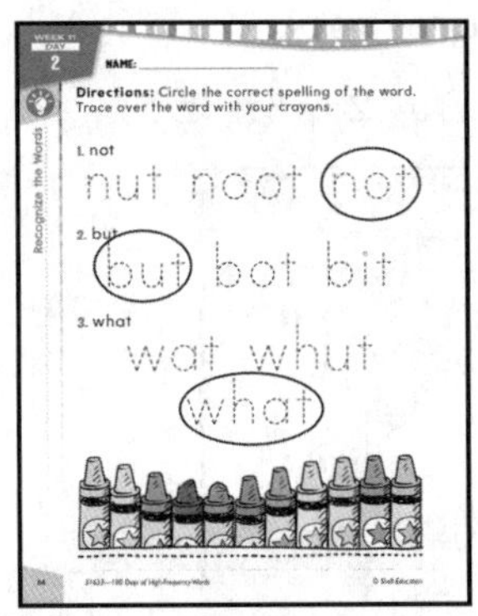
NAME:

Directions: Circle the correct spelling of the word. Trace over the word with your crayons.

1. not
nut noot not

2. but
but bot bit

3. what
wat whut what

Week 11: Day 4 (page 66)

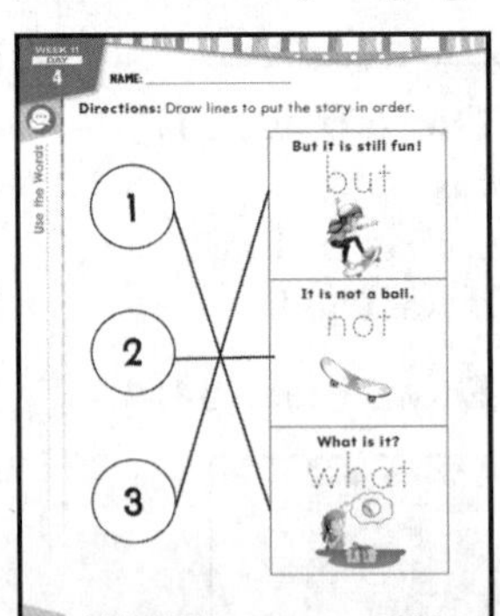
NAME:

Directions: Draw lines to put the story in order.

1 2 3

But it is still fun!
but

It is not a ball.
not

What is it?
what

Week 5: Day 5 (page 67)

He asked, "<u>What</u> is this?" This is <u>not</u> a bike. <u>But</u> it is still fun.

Week 12: Day 2 (page 69)

NAME:

Directions: Read each word. Find the hidden word. Circle the hidden word.

we all were

tpekwajwurbhswe
kstheksIbIlalualleu
wtiwereksuwerksn

Week 12: Day 4 (page 71)

1. **We** love you.
2. I see **all** the pets.
3. **Were** you sad?

Week 13: Day 2 (page 74)

NAME:

Directions: Read each word. Draw lines between the matching words.

can — can
your — your
when — when

Week 13: Day 4 (page 76)

1. I **can** skip.
2. **When** is Monday?
3. **Your** mom waves.

Week 14: Day 2 (page 79)

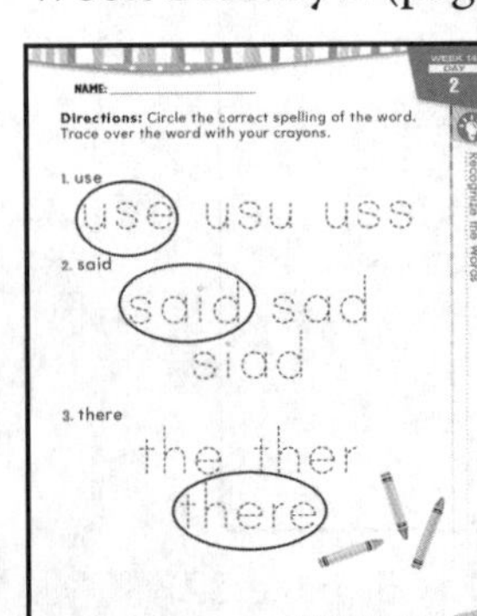
NAME:

Directions: Circle the correct spelling of the word. Trace over the word with your crayons.

1. use
use usu uss

2. said
said sad siad

3. there
the ther there

ANSWER KEY *(cont.)*

Week 14: Day 4 (page 81)

Week 14: Day 5 (page 82)

She said, "There is a ball?
Let's use it to play."

Week 15: Day 2 (page 84)

Week 15: Day 4 (page 86)

1. Here is **a**n apple.
2. E**a**ch kid has a ball.
3. Wh**i**ch one do you like?

Week 16: Day 2 (page 89)

Week 16: Day 4 (page 91)

1. I can **do** my work.
2. Can **she** see you?
3. Look **how** fast it goes.

Week 17: Day 2 (page 94)

Week 17: Day 4 (page 96)

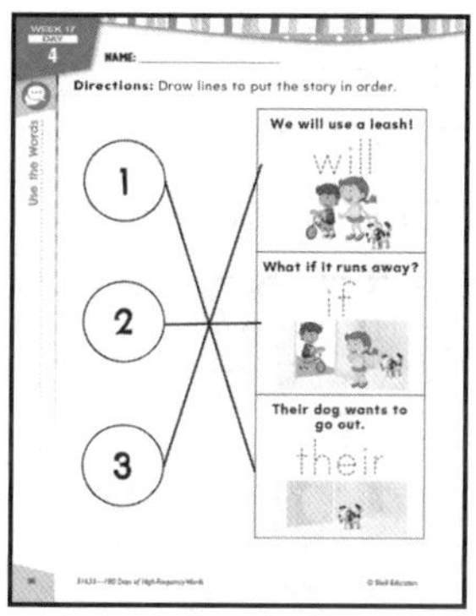

Week 17: Day 5 (page 97)

What will they name their dog?
I would name it Jax if I could.

Week 18 Day 2 (page 99)

Week 18: Day 4 (page 101)

1. The rat is **u**p on top.
2. What ab**o**ut me?
3. Do you see the oth**e**r kids?

Week 19: Day 1 (page 103)

Week 19: Day 2 (page 104)

Week 19: Day 4 (page 105)

1. Look **out**!
2. I have **many** pets.
3. I will go home **then**.

Week 20: Day 2 (page 109)

Week 20: Day 4 (page 111)

1. Th**e**se bags are big.
2. Can you see th**e**m?
3. The sun is **s**o hot!

ANSWER KEY *(cont.)*

Week 21: Day 2 (page 114)

Directions: Circle the correct spelling of the word. Trace over the word with your crayons.

1. would — wold woud would
2. some — sume some soo
3. her — her har here

Week 21: Day 3 (page 115)

1. would
2. her
3. some

Week 21: Day 4 (page 116)

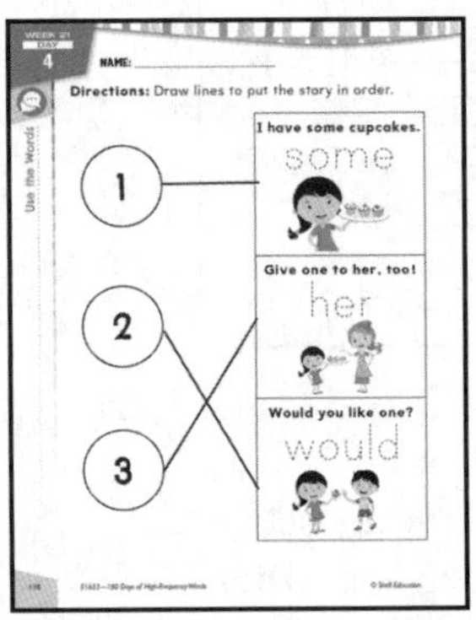
Directions: Draw lines to put the story in order.

I have some cupcakes. — some

Give one to her, too! — her

Would you like one? — would

Week 22: Day 2 (page 119)

Directions: Read each word. Find the hidden word. Circle the hidden word.

him like make

skekhimhsixoakmeis

hikshehnmkshelikesl

khmilskmakeishlqng

Week 22: Day 4 (page 121)

1. I sat with **him**.
2. We **like** ice cream.
3. Let's **make** a snowman!

Week 23: Day 2 (page 124)

Directions: Look at the shape of the word. Find the box with that shape. Write each letter in a box.

time has into

Example: boy

1. has
2. into
3. time

Week 23: Day 4 (page 126)

1. He **has** a snake.
2. What **time** is it?
3. Go **into** the house.

Week 24: Day 2 (page 129)

Directions: Read each word. Draw lines between the matching words.

look — two

two — more

more — look

Week 24: Day 3 (page 130)

1. more
2. two
3. look

Week 24: Day 4 (page 131)

1. I have one <u>more</u> candy left.
2. The cat has <u>two</u> kittens.
3. <u>Look</u> at the rainbow.

Week 25: Day 2 (page 134)

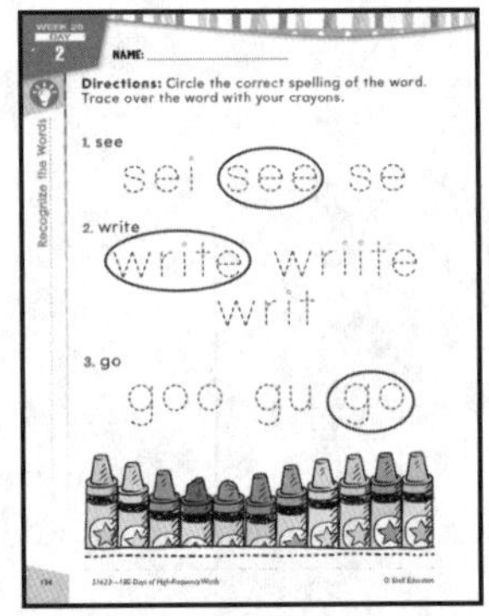
Directions: Circle the correct spelling of the word. Trace over the word with your crayons.

1. see — sei see se
2. write — write wriite writ
3. go — goo gu go

Week 25: Day 4 (page 136)

1. I can **write** my name.
2. Let's **go** to the park.
3. I **see** my mom.

Week 26: Day 1 (page 138)

Directions: Read the sentences. Circle the word in each sentence. Write each word.

number no way

This is house number one. number

No one is home. no

Let's go this way. way

Week 26: Day 2 (page 139)

Directions: Read each word. Find each hidden word twice. Circle the hidden words.

no number way

disnoskenlkswyaois

kshenumberlsksoke

skdjwaylkzumborks

ANSWER KEY *(cont.)*

Week 26: Day 4 (page 141)

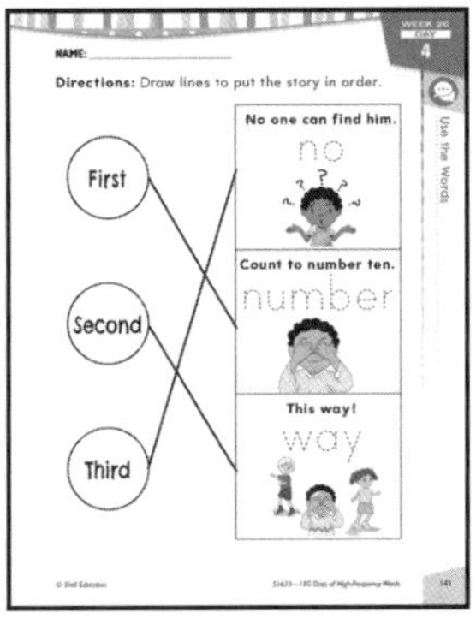

Week 27: Day 2 (page 144)

Week 27: Day 4 (page 146)

1. **M**y cat is black.
2. The peo**p**le are tall.
3. Cou**l**d you see me?

Week 28: Day 2 (page 149)

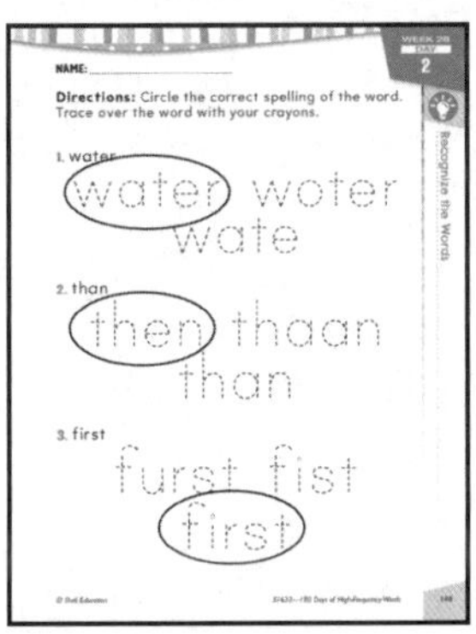

Week 28: Day 4 (page 151)

1. The water is very cold.
2. I won first place.
3. I am taller than my brother.

Week 29: Day 2 (page 154)

Week 29: Day 4 (page 156)

1. **Who** is Jose?
2. He is making a **call.**
3. It has **been** raining.

Week 30: Day 1 (page 158)

Week 30: Day 2 (page 159)

Week 30: Day 3 (page 160)

1. all
2. find
3. now

Week 30: Day 4 (page 161)

1. I love **all** of my family.
2. I can't f**i**nd my hat!
3. I want to go n**o**w.

Week 31: Day 2 (page 164)

Week 31: Day 4 (page 166)

1. It is a hot **day**.
2. Go **down** the slide.
3. My hair is **long**.

Week 32: Day 2 (page 169)

Week 32: Day 4 (page 171)

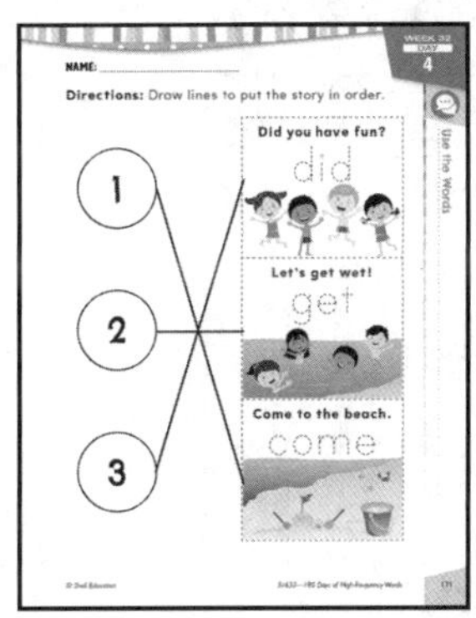

ANSWER KEY *(cont.)*

Week 33: Day 1 (page 173)

NAME:

Directions: Read the sentences. Circle the word in each sentence. Write each word three times.

may made from

This vase is made of glass.

made made made

It is from my grandma.

from from from

May I hold it?

may may may

Week 33: Day 2 (page 174)

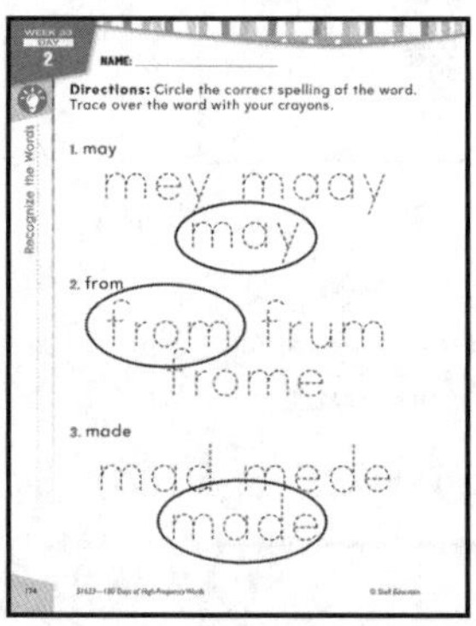
NAME:

Directions: Circle the correct spelling of the word. Trace over the word with your crayons.

1. may

mey maay may

2. from

from frum frome

3. made

mad mede made

Week 33: Day 3 (page 175)

1. may
2. made
3. from

Week 33: Day 4 (page 176)

1. My dad picks me up from school.
2. We made posters today.
3. May I have more food?

Week 34: Day 2 (page 179)

NAME:

Directions: Look at the shape of the word. Find the box with that shape. Write each letter in a box.

part what over

Example: bank

1. over

2. part

3. what

Week 34: Day 4 (page 181)

1. What **part** do you want?
2. Her hand is **over** my hand.
3. Do you know **what** time is it?

Week 35: Day 2 (page 184)

NAME:

Directions: Read each word. Find each hidden word twice. Circle the hidden words.

many be said

saidkbekshmanyx

ksudlbmanyskben

kslgjskbeupsaidsv

Week 35: Day 4 (page 186)

1. I ma**d**e my bed.
2. The w**a**ter is warm.
3. My dog di**d** it!

Week 36: Day 2 (page 189)

NAME:

Directions: Read each word. Draw lines between the matching words.

other look

look would

would other

Week 36: Day 4 (page 191)

1. **Their** shoes were wet.
2. We **were** skating.
3. I am **about** to go to bed.

HOME/SCHOOL CONNECTIONS AND EXTENSION ACTIVITIES

Pages 199–206 can be used as home/school connection activities for additional practice or classroom extension activities. All game sheets have been left blank so the teacher can differentiate for each individual student and/or group in the class. The flash cards on pages 207–215 can be used as game cards, as well as student-facing assessment cards for quarterly assessments.

BINGO

Write the high-frequency words of the week (or ones that need to be practiced) on the BINGO board. Select a word from the deck of flash cards. Any player who has the word can place a chip on it. The first player to make a straight line calls out "Bingo!"

		FREE SPACE		

HOME/SCHOOL CONNECTIONS AND EXTENSION ACTIVITIES *(cont.)*

Race to 10! Race to 20!

Give each student a whiteboard or notepad to serve as a scoreboard. Use the flash cards from pages 207–215 to create a card pile for this game. Pick a card from the flash card pile, read the word, and count the letters in the word. Add a tally mark for each letter. Take turns picking cards, reading words, and adding up tally marks. The first player to reach 10 tally marks wins! As a challenge, Race to 20!

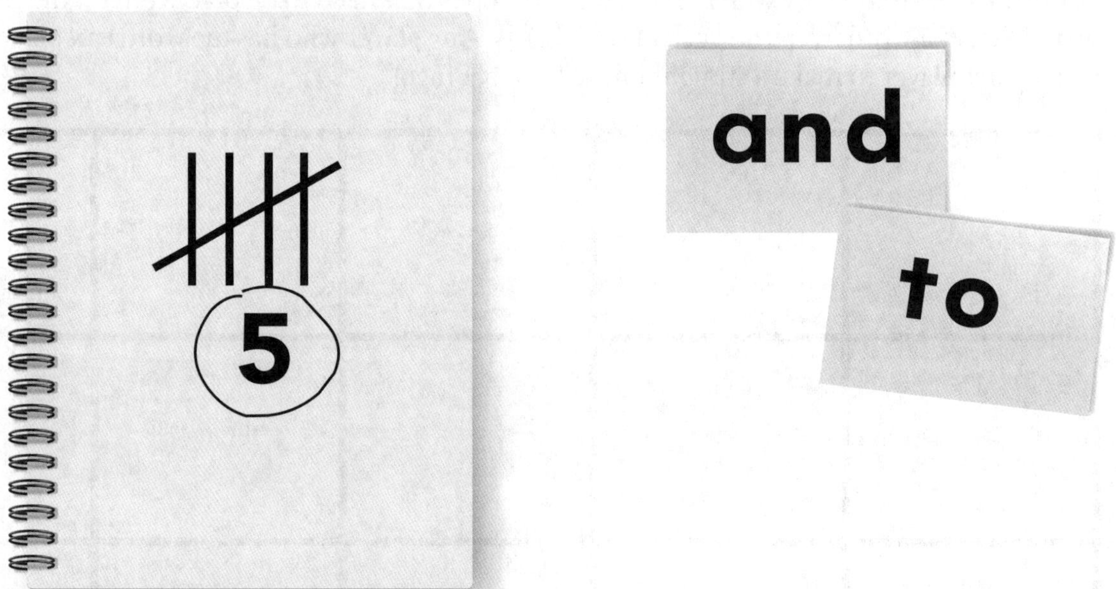

HOME/SCHOOL CONNECTIONS AND EXTENSION ACTIVITIES *(cont.)*

Word Board Game

Choose several words and place those flash cards in a pile. Write the words multiple times on the game board until all spaces are filled. Then, distribute a chip to each player. Have each player select a flash card, count the number of letters in the word, and then move his or her chip that number of spaces. Have students read every space they land on. The first player to reach the finish line wins!

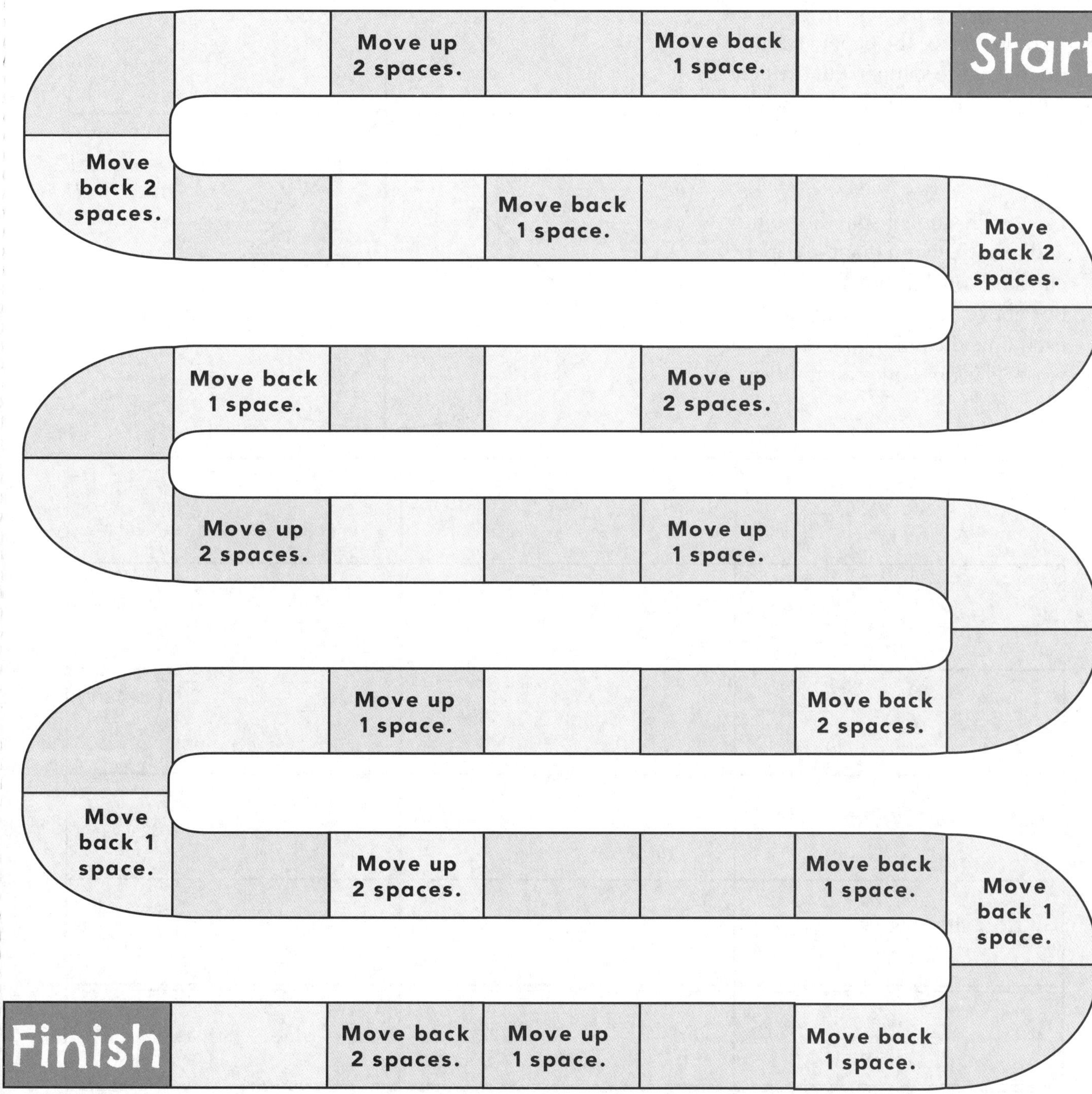

HOME/SCHOOL CONNECTIONS AND EXTENSION ACTIVITIES *(cont.)*

Word Bar Graph

Write the words of the week multiple times in the spinner. Write the words of the week on the lines at the bottom of the graph.

Use a paper clip and pencil to make a pointer. Place the paper clip in the middle of the spinner. Put the pencil inside of the paper clip so when it is spun, the paper clip circles around the pencil.

Have each student spin the pointer and read the word that the paper clip lands on. Starting from the box above the word, fill in one box each time the pointer lands on that word. Play until one column reaches the top.

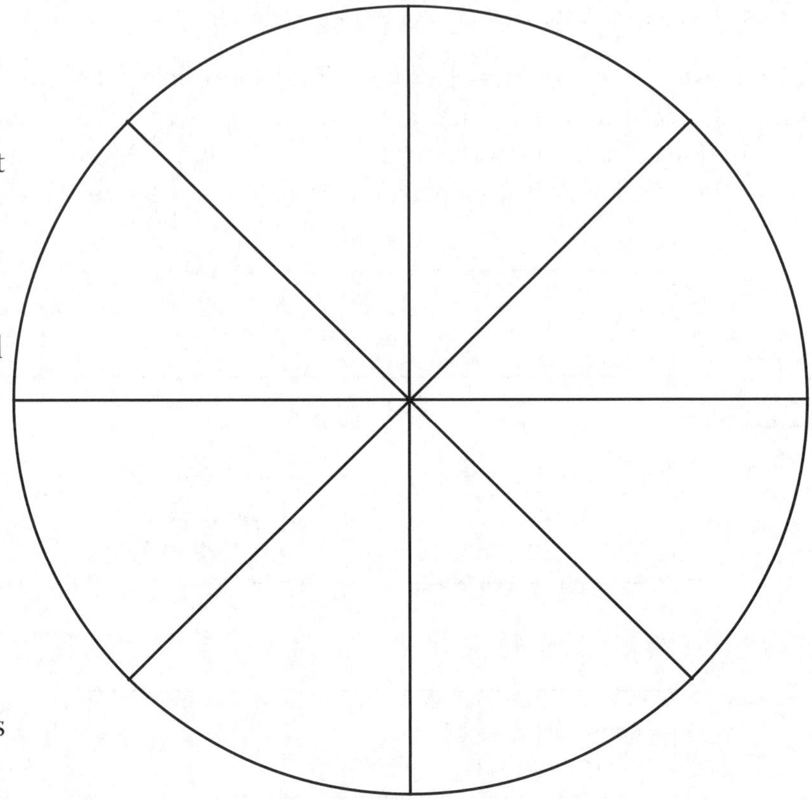

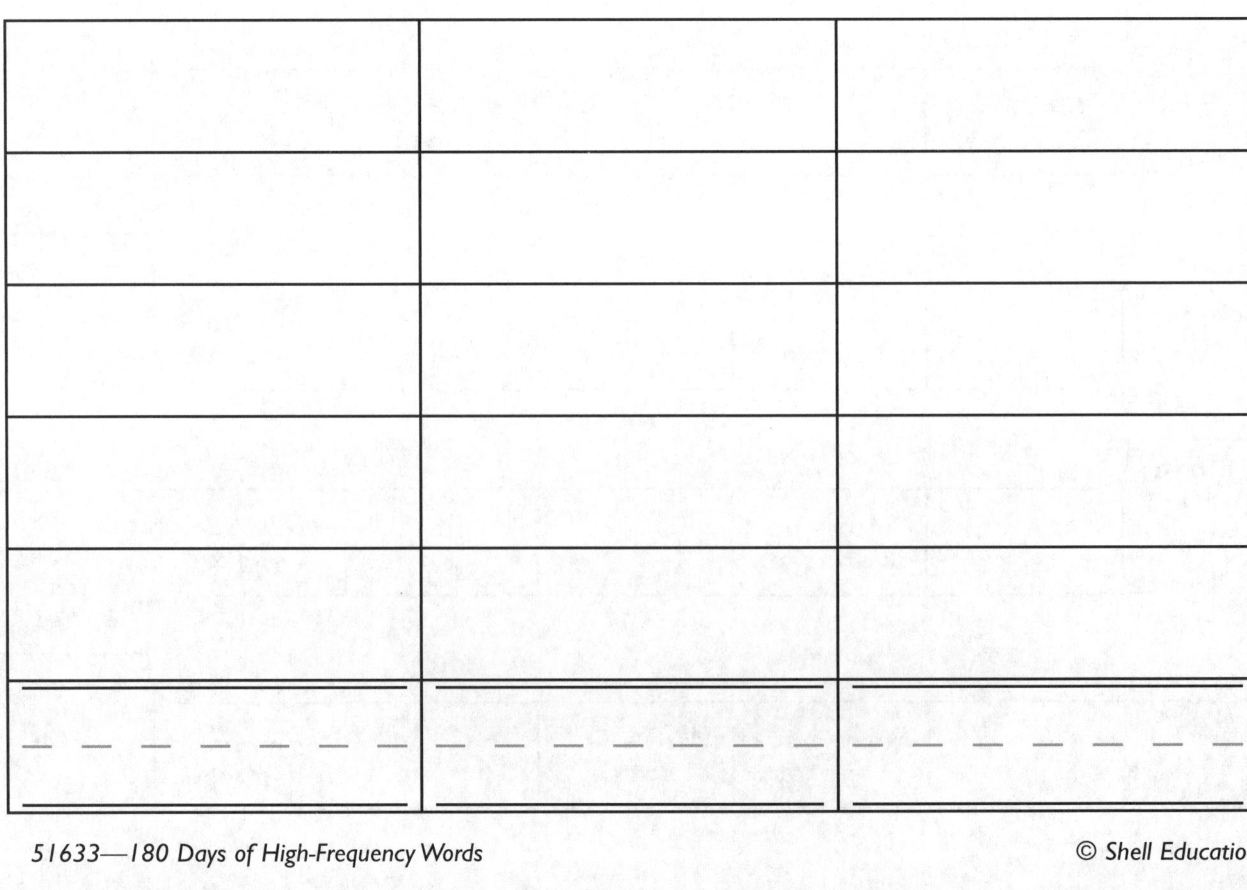

HOME/SCHOOL CONNECTIONS AND EXTENSION ACTIVITIES *(cont.)*

Tally It Up!

Select six words, and write them in the second column. Have each student roll a die 20 times. For each roll, students say the word associated with each number, then color one tally mark. For each roll have students color one box next to the word that matches the number rolled. To liven up the game, instruct students to say each word in a normal voice and a strange one.

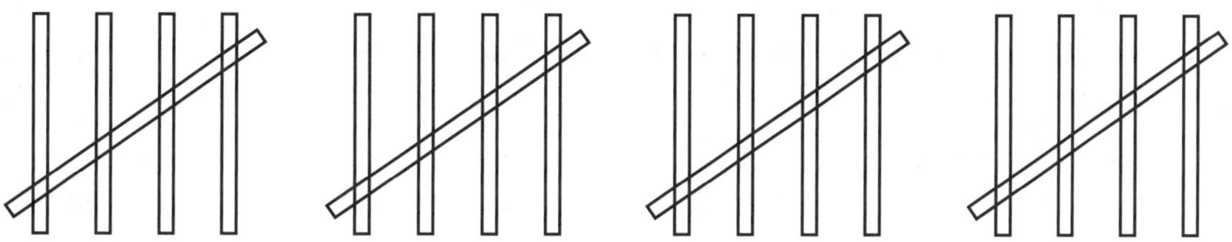

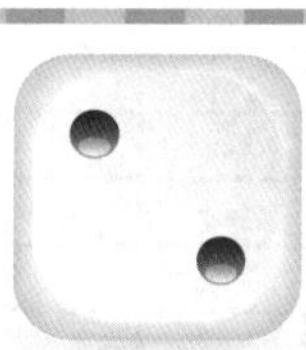									
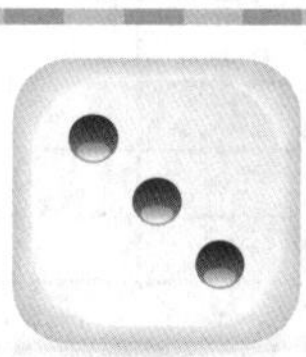									
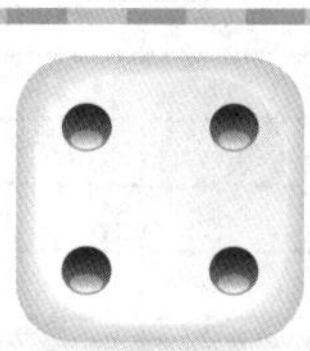									
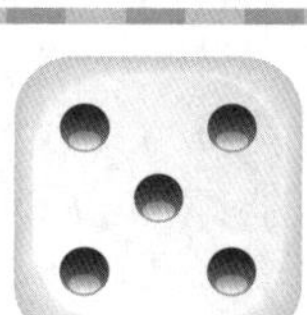									
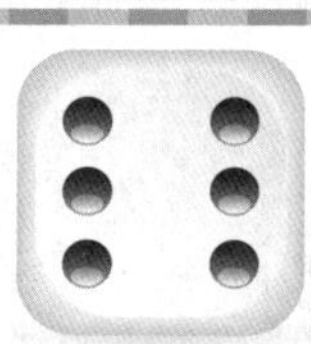									

HOME/SCHOOL CONNECTIONS AND EXTENSION ACTIVITIES *(cont.)*

Scavenger Hunt for the Print-Rich Classroom

Have students take a classroom walk to find some of the words of the week. When students find a word, have them stand next to it. This game can be differentiated to include the following hunts:

- Find a word in the classroom that starts with the same sound as . . .
- Find a word in the classroom that ends with the same sound as . . .
- Find a word in the classroom that starts/ends with the same letter as . . .
- Find a word in the classroom that has the same syllable count as . . .
- Find a word in the classroom that has the same amount of letters as . . .
- Find a word in the classroom that has the same about of vowels/consonants as . . .

Tiny-Print Word Search

Use the chart below to find the high-frequency words of the week. Give each student a magnifying glass. Use the list on page 11 to call out each high-frequency word. **Note:** All of the words in this book are listed below multiple times!

the	than	my	had	all	said	she	by	if	of	word	could	their	were	not
there	may	come	but	and	what	will	them	her	a	we	did	time	out	an
to	the	and	how	other	him	in	look	people	no	is	over	call	look	like
that	you	about	two	write	down	you	first	day	long	go	was	it	been	see
about	that	first	he	find	some	could	now	was	this	part	would	made	have	and
for	were	water	number	which	use	what	there	were	the	to	I	that	get	in
on	day	his	water	from	of	a	is	come	you	be	number	they	I	have
make	there	of	all	a	was	are	be	said	that	one	these	with	as	water
has	but	how	made	did	with	she	these	use	been	people	so	his	make	may
many	over	what	that	look	get	I	cover	so	other	would	who	at	my	each
two	from	no	be	than	when	who	this	find	about	more	with	have	write	then
from	up	or	or	do	would	your	one	way	who	up	have	also	into	can
to	said	way	you	it	he	for	on	his	they	at	one	an	for	on
are	has	part	as	had	by	word	not	can	your	when	long	each	which	do
their	day	down	if	up	out	then	some	like	him	her	first	many	will	how
them	call	now	these	time	has	into	more	go	no	way	other	number	see	so

HOME/SCHOOL CONNECTIONS AND EXTENSION ACTIVITIES *(cont.)*

Guess My Word

Print the flash cards on pages 207–215. Have students work in pairs. One partner should hold a flash card to his or her forehead while the other partner gives the clues. Once the partner guesses the word correctly, the other student takes a turn. Students can use any of the prompts below as clues:

- "The word has ______ syllables."
- "The word rhymes with ______."
- "The word has ______ vowels."
- "The word has ______ consonants."
- "The word has ______ letters."
- Use the word in a sentence. For example: "______ is coming to your party?"

Dance and Write

Give every pair of students a dry-erase board and marker. Play some music. When the music stops, call out a word. The first team to write the word on their board and hold it up gets the point.

Dance, Tally, and Graph

As an alternative to Dance and Write, remove the competitive aspect. Give every student a clipboard and a sheet of paper. Have students write the words of the week on their paper. Play music, and when the music stops call out a word. Have students write a tally mark next to every word called. When students reach five tally marks for every word, repeat the game/song.

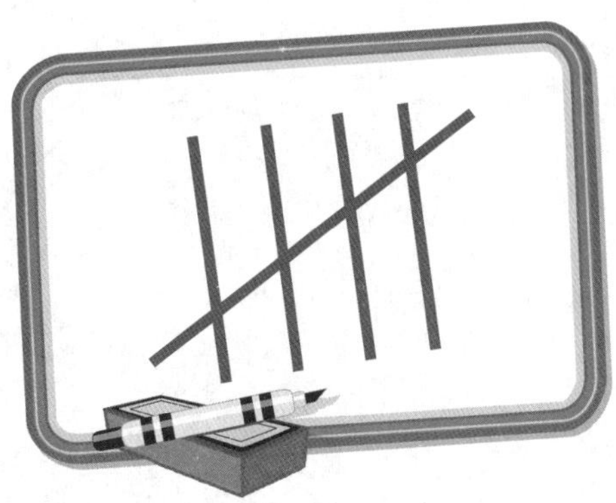

HOME/SCHOOL CONNECTIONS AND EXTENSION ACTIVITIES *(cont.)*

Ice Cream Word Sort

Choose a sorting category for students, and write it on the cone. Using the flash cards from pages 207–215, have students select and write words that fit the sort onto each scoop of ice cream. Have students color the ice cream once complete. Sorting categories can be found on pages 204–205.

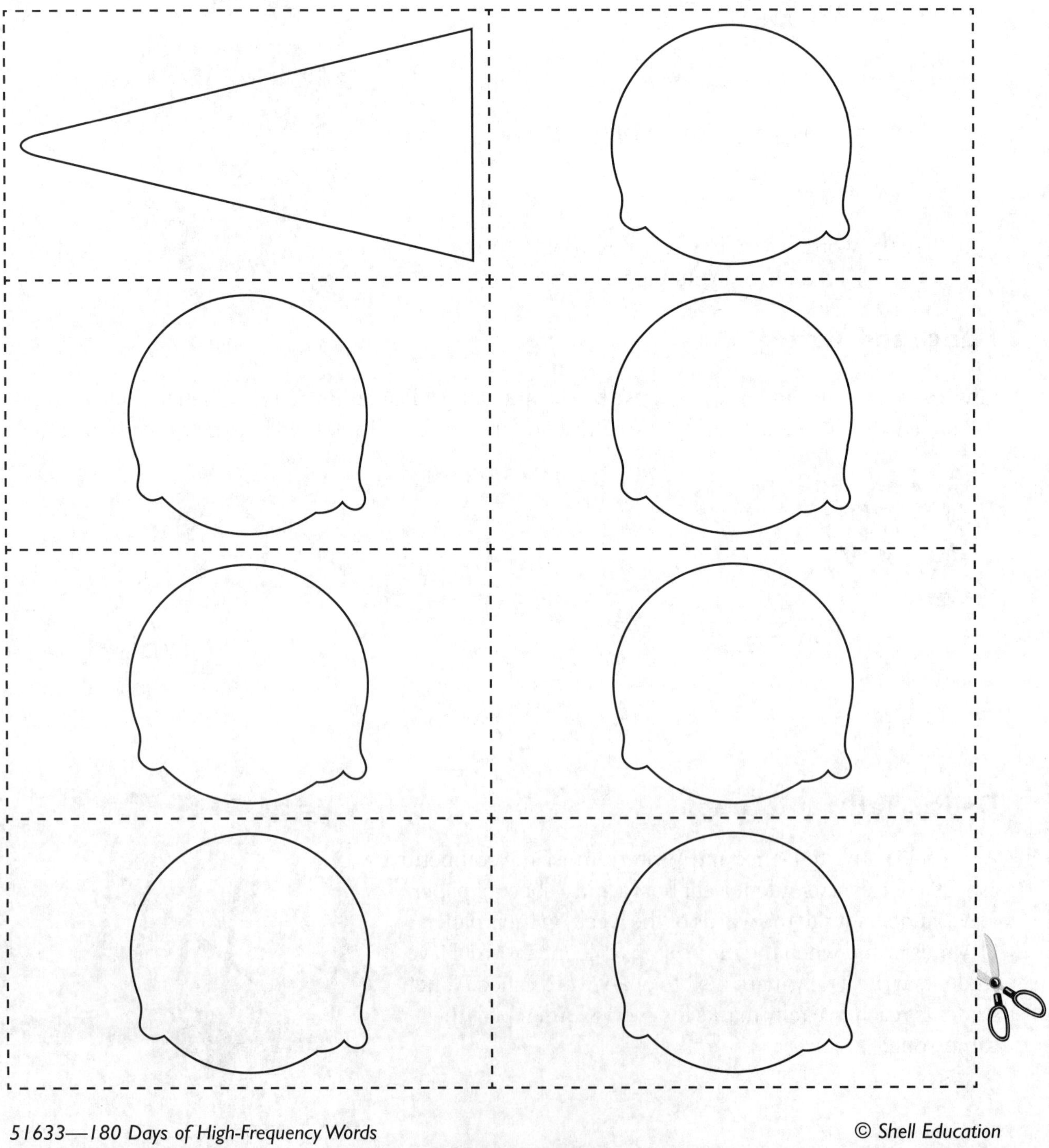

HIGH-FREQUENCY WORDS FLASH CARDS

The flash cards on pages 207–215 are organized by week. **Note:** If you are using the cards for the student diagnostic assessment, have students read the words left to right, as they would read text in a book. Below you will find weeks 1–3.

and	in	you
of	to	that
the	a	is

HIGH-FREQUENCY WORDS FLASH CARDS *(cont.)*

Below you will find weeks 4–7.

was | are | his | at

he | on | with | I

it | for | as | they

HIGH-FREQUENCY WORDS FLASH CARDS *(cont.)*

Below you will find weeks 8–11.

have	one	word	what
this	or	by	but
be	from	had	not

HIGH-FREQUENCY WORDS FLASH CARDS *(cont.)*

Below you will find weeks 12–15.

were	when	there	which
all	your	said	each
we	can	use	an

HIGH-FREQUENCY WORDS FLASH CARDS *(cont.)*

Below you will find weeks 16–19.

how	will	about	then
do	if	other	many
she	their	up	out

HIGH-FREQUENCY WORDS FLASH CARDS *(cont.)*

Below you will find weeks 20–23.

so	would	him	into
these	her	like	has
them	some	make	time

HIGH-FREQUENCY WORDS FLASH CARDS *(cont.)*

Below you will find weeks 24–27.

more	see	way	my
two	go	no	people
look	write	number	could

HIGH-FREQUENCY WORDS FLASH CARDS *(cont.)*

Below you will find weeks 28–31.

water	who	find	down
first	call	now	day
than	been	all	long

HIGH-FREQUENCY WORDS FLASH CARDS *(cont.)*

Below you will find weeks 32–34.

come	from	what
get	may	over
did	made	part

REFERENCES CITED

Fry, Edward. 2000. *1,000 Instant Words: The Most Common Words for Teaching Reading, Writing, and Spelling.* Huntington Beach, CA: Teacher Created Materials.

Marzano, Robert. 2010. "When Practice Makes Perfect…Sense." Educational Leadership 68 (3): 81–83.

McIntosh, Margaret E. 1997. "Formative Assessment in Mathematics." *The Clearing House: A Journal of Educational Strategies* 71 (2): 92–96.

US Department of Health and Human Services. 2000. *Report of the National Reading Panel: Teaching Children to Read: An Evidence-Based Assessment of the Scientific Research Literature on Reading and its Implications for Reading Instruction.* Washington, DC: US Government Printing Office.

CONTENTS OF THE DIGITAL RESOURCES

Teacher Resources

Resource	PDF Filename	Microsoft Word® Filename
Daily Descriptions	daily.pdf	daily.docx
Activity Descriptions	activity.pdf	activity.docx
Student Item Analysis Checklist	studentlog.pdf	studentlog.docx
Class Item Analysis	classlog.pdf	classlog.docx
Standards Chart	standards.pdf	

Student Resources

Resource	PDF Filename
Bingo Board	bingo.pdf
Word Board Game	boardgame.pdf
Word Bar Graph	wordgraph.pdf
Spinner	spinner.pdf
Tally It Up!	tally.pdf
Tiny-Print Word Search	tinysearch.pdf
Ice Cream Word Sort	icecream.pdf
High-Frequency Words Flash Cards	flashcards.pdf